HEYDAYS

Works by Alister Kershaw written in France

Accent & Hazard (1951)
Murder in France (1955)
A History of the Guillotine (1958)
Heydays (1991)
A Word from Paris (1991)
Village to Village (1993)
Collected Poems (1993)
Complete Poems of Mort Brandish (1994)
A Second Denunciad (1994)
One for the Road (2003)

IMPRINT
CLASSICS

HEYDAYS

**A Glimpse of
Melbourne's Bohemia 1937-1947**

—

ALISTER KERSHAW

Introduced by
GRAEME BLUNDELL

ETT IMPRINT

SYDNEY-PARIS LINK

This edition published by ETT Imprint, Exile Bay 2025

First published by Angus & Robertson in 1991

First electronic edition published by ETT Imprint 2017

ETT IPRINT
PO Box R1906
Royal Exchange NSW 1225
Australia

ISBN 978-1-923205-74-1 (paper)
ISBN 978-1-922698-14-8 (ebook)

Design and frontispiece by Tom Thompson

Cover and all photographs by Albert Tucker.

A Sydney-Paris Link publication
in memory of Jean-Paul Delamotte

For Peter Higginson

Alister Naysmith Kershaw, Melbourne 1937.

FOREWORD

Poor unloved Melbourne! It never got a civil word from us. It's architecture was obnoxious, the climate was inclined to be peevish, you couldn't buy a drink after six p.m. (unless you were dining in a restaurant when you could have a high old time right up to eight p.m.), the tiniest deviation from conformity in the way you dressed earned you some filthy looks, and we writers and painters and composers weren't treated with the respect we deserved."

This is the way Alister Kershaw introduces his delightful and witty memoir *Heydays*, a personal record of cultural Melbourne in the thirties and forties. And the pages that follow display a account of the bohemia of his youth and tribute to such friends and mentors as the exuberant Max Harris, Adrian Lawlor, whose unique character defied description, and Albert Tucker, "The only intellectual with any brains."

It's a lovely, disrespectful part of our collective archive, as was Alister Kershaw himself. As with endangered birds, the last "hearings" of Melbourne's remaining bohemians became increasingly infrequent, and with Kershaw's death in 1995, at Maison Salle, Cher, in France, they disappeared.

As Peter Coleman said in his obituary of this charming character, he liked to joke that future pedants would treat him as some sort of mysterious Dark Lady of the Sonnets. "Did he really exist?" they would ask.

They would find some clues, the obituarist suggested. Roy Campbell dedicated a poem to him. Ezra Pound mentioned him in his letters. Richard Aldington said that his Lawrence of Arabia was Kershaw's idea. But his early poetry was neglected, and, in the end, he insisted, the literary establishment would decide that he was a private joke, an invention like Woody Allen's *Zelig*.

So, this new publication of *Heydays* is a rare anthropological treat, transporting us somewhat magically to a city he looks back on in his dotage, "With an affection I was too brash to experience at the time".

I met him once, not long before he died, while he was in Australia promoting his collection of radio broadcasts from the sixties, when he provided Australians with hot news from France with his twice weekly broadcasts for the ABC.

And I was fascinated to meet someone who was a footnote to cultural history, and who with Max Harris, Sidney Nolan, Albert Tucker, James Gleeson, Adrian Lawlor, Gino Nibbi, John and Sunday Reed and all the other rebels and precursors fought to establish "the freak of modernism", as their opponents called it. Those heydays were fun for some.

"Well, it was all joy," Max Harris wrote in *The Bulletin* forty years later, "all a sort of morning glory in the springtime of the mind. We were a closed society, a comradeship, surrounded by enemies and potential destroyers."

Kershaw was a passionate partisan in those days, but always a humorous one, often remembered for almost Dadaesque stunts. Once at a lecture at Melbourne university he drew on a pair of white gloves before handling a copy of the *Worker's Voice*, reading aloud from it, and berating Marxism. He also read two surrealist poems by James Gleeson backwards. No-one recalls which event caused the most offence.

"I lived in Carlton in one of those tiny attic-garret's", Kershaw said sitting in a bamboo chair in the Lounge Bar on the first floor of The Holiday Inn, formerly Sydney's famous Menzies Hotel, one hand holding a glass, the other waving to a waiter to get one for me. "I thought this was High Romance. I can still remember the first artist's studio I ever set foot in. I was seventeen. I remember thinking this was something. This was Bohemia. Of course it was naive, but I think you ought to always be a bit naive in that way."

Melbourne's actual Bohemia, he writes in *Heydays*, was fifty square yards at the top of Little Collins Street, -"where you could wear corduroy trousers without being taken for a poofter and where the sight of a beard didn t provoke a display of popular indignation. You could even get away with sandals."

Speaking in almost courtly prose, with perfect sentences and beautifully timed pauses, he presented himself as a bit of a dreamer and drifter in a savage place just passing through. Naivety was not however, the first word that comes to mind on meeting Alister Kershaw.

The worst informer, according to Proverbs, is the face. The beauty of one is supposed to have launched a thousand ships. Owners of those less endowed have thought of suing their parents for damages. Suffering hypochondriacs offer it like the visiting card of their general constitution. Embossed as it is with the state of their health, it becomes a map depicting ridges, valleys, cracks, and lines caused by the joys, upheavals, aches and pains of time.

Kershaw was no hypochondriac and was a man of few regrets, but the angles, planes and hollows of his head suggested he had seldom deviated from an old bohemian's duty of subversion.

"In our day the whole idea was not to toe any line. Now everyone's got to have a cause," he said with the survivor's sense of the sadness of contemporary life.

"Writers are judged on the basis of where they stand, not for what they write. Then, apart from the communists, I don't think anyone gave a damn about politics. We despised politicians, which I still do - extreme left, extreme right and all those passing by in the centre. We realised we were likely to suffer from politics in one form or another, but we also knew there was nothing to be done about it, so we just got on with our work."

Even at seventy, he delighted in provoking a response, though he did it then with world-weary indifference and an almost Wodehousian High Tory charm. Being provocative was harder in the forties. Extreme censorship cramped the young poet-provocateur's style somewhat. Kershaw says it was hard to know which official actually chose their reading matter.

"I have an idea it was the Postmaster-General, but it may just as easily have been the Minister for Agriculture, or the Chairman of the State Railways, or the Secretary of the Wharf Labourer's Union," he writes in *Heydays*. "We weren't allowed to read anything more sexually stimulating than Winnie-The-Pooh and writers were all but forbidden to use ANY word that began with F."

Fifty years later in the Lounge Bar, he opened another packet of Gitanes and ordered more Pirramimma chardonnay, daring the wowsers out of the heavily lacquered woodwork.

It was a long way from the pubs he describes in *Heydays*. "They were the closest thing to lazar-houses since the Middle Ages," he writes, referencing those places that once housed lepers. "You took your life in your hands whenever you ordered a beer. It was good beer but the way it was served was something you had to get accustomed to. I doubt if anyone had the nerve to ask for a clean glass."

I'm glad I met him. An afternoon with Alister Kershaw, like his beguiling memoir, was filled with comic scenes and memorable characters.

In *Heydays*, he draws humour from his defeats and weaknesses, and occasional small triumphs, with the sort of mandarin sense of knowing when to move on to the next story that you don't often come across these days.

It's a bit like being presented with a huge plate of assorted and fascinating-looking canapes at some exotic party. The only way to go is to pick and choose and resist the temptation to polish off the whole lot in one go.

Graeme Blundell

Acknowledgment

A number of people have given a nudge to what is left of my memory or have helped in other ways with the writing of this book. With the usual proviso that they deserve no blame whatsoever for the contents, I extend my sincere thanks to Christopher Connolly, Patricia Davies, Geoffrey Dutton, Geoff Jones, Sylvain and Annie Kershaw, Jelka Kozmus, John Murphy, Justin O'Brien, Desmond O'Grady, Nicholas Pounder, Stephen Rantz and Albert Tucker. A.K.

Albert Tucker, aged 25, in 1940.

Introduction

Poor unloved Melbourne! It never got a civil word from us. Its architecture was obnoxious, the climate was inclined to be peevish, you couldn't buy a drink after six p.m. (unless you were dining in a restaurant when you could have a high old time right up to eight p.m.), the tiniest deviation from conformity in the way you dressed earned you some very dirty looks, and we writers and painters and composers weren't treated with the respect we deserved. If the place didn't pull itself together, we told each other, one of these days we'd up-anchor and go somewhere where we'd be appreciated and Melbourne would just have to try to get on without us.

Well, some of our complaints were justified - no question of that; and some weren't. The drinking hours might have been a bit hard to take but later on some of us would find that, at any rate, the beer (when you could get to it) beat the stuff they served in London and Paris by miles. The shortcomings of the architecture could be matched in any other city. And compared to what went on in Europe, the climate was that of a tropic isle. Maybe artists weren't looked upon with holy dread (we never asked ourselves why the hell they should be) but at least they were left alone. By the public, that is. Now and again, some artist of the old school would reach the end of his tether and start mumbling about decadence and incompetence and fraud and we *avant-garde* kids occasionally roughed each other up a bit; but that was as far as it went. In Paris, the rival schools practically used knuckle-dusters on each other. French artists spent more time warding off attacks from the enemy camp than they did actually painting or writing.

When you came down to it, the official censorship in Melbourne (and everywhere else in Australia unless Norfolk Island had been overlooked) was the worst we had to contend with. That was plenty, however. We weren't allowed to read anything more sexually stimulating than Winnie-the-Pooh and writers were all but forbidden to use any word that began with F.

But the truth is that Melbourne, on the whole, was a pretty good spot and in my dotage I look back on it with an affection I was too brash to experience at the time. And it did, after all, harbour some blithe spirits who would have made any city worth living in the fabulous (and I could add a dozen other adjectives and still not convey his unique character) Adrian Lawlor; the ebullient Max Harris; the tempestuous Denison Deasey; David Strachan, combining a luminous poetic vision with a splendidly scatological vocabulary; Albert Tucker, the only intellectual with any brains; and quite a few more. It had its Rogues' Gallery too, to my way of thinking the heresy-hunting Noel Counihan, the schoolmasterly John Reed - but they'll all be cropping up in due course.

These are some of the people I've tried to recall in this book If you find it heavy going, it's my fault, not theirs.

Alister Kershaw
1991

ONE

Back in the Thirties and early Forties there were about fifty square yards at the top of Melbourne's Little Collins Street where you could wear corduroy trousers without being taken for a poofter and where the sight of a beard didn't provoke a display of popular indignation. You could even get away with sandals. The bewitching young artist Alannah Coleman could get away with more than that. Her costume was, as a rule, richly international. Once when we were having dinner together, she arrived wearing velvet trousers and a Breton fisherman's striped shirt. A cape like those worn by officers of the Bersaglieri hung to her ankles. An Egyptian fez was perched becomingly on her long blonde hair. A quiver of arrows slung over her shoulders added a Robin Hood or Saxon touch. If she had anything on her feet at all, it can only have been a pair of Roman sandals. Anywhere else in the city, she might have been run in on a charge of disturbing the peace; here, she received no more attention than was due to an exceptionally attractive young woman.

There was a tremendously exotic cafe, the Petrushka, which was important to us. The Monte Carlo Ballet Company had settled more or less permanently in Melbourne and had gone straight to our heads. We were determined Slavophiles. Some of us learnt to say *dasvidanya* and said it whenever we got a chance. When Sidney Nolan was commissioned to do the decor for a new ballet by Lichine, we ached with jealousy. It was as if he had been made an honorary cadet in the Preobrajensky Guards. The Petrushka was the only place where tea was served in glasses. We didn't need any more than that to make us happy.

A seedy restaurant which we used to frequent laid on a memorably horrible meal for fifty cents. The solid citizens may have looked on us as an effete lot but I'd like to have seen them try to swallow the grisly morsels which were served up there. You had to be tough to manage it. The price included a small carafe of wine. That was what kept our custom. It came as close to being undrinkable as was permitted by the laws of God and man and we would have much preferred to drink beer anyway. But if tea in glasses was Old Saint Petersburg, wine on the table was Paris in the springtime and, as far as we were concerned, the next best thing to being Russian was being French.

There were a couple of art galleries in this Bohemian enclave and a couple of artists' studios. With the sandals and corduroy trousers, the Petrushka and that carafe of wine on the table, it all added up to our own antipodean Chelsea, our Greenwich Village, our St Germain des Pres. Bang in the middle of it was Gino Nibbi's Leonardo Bookshop.

We venerated Gino. He was the boss. None of us really knew why. He had a number of engaging characteristics but charm has never been required of oracles, rather the contrary. He was prodigiously cultivated but there were several other bright boys in the neighbourhood. It certainly wasn't an irresistible determination to dominate the scene which endowed him with his unaccountable authority. Nobody could have been less self-assertive. Still, there it was. We didn't give a damn what anyone else thought of us but we candidly hankered after Gino's good opinion. However much or however well you wrote or painted or sculpted or composed, unless you had Gino's okay you didn't qualify as any sort of artist, not even in your own eyes. Acceptance by Gino wasn't signified by so much as a public pat on the back but somehow the news got around. From then on, you were taken seriously.

Initiates - Albert Tucker, say, or George Bell, or Adrian Lawlor - rarely let a week go by without visiting Gino at the Leonardo. They - we - went there to riffle through books in languages we couldn't read and to look at reproductions of painters we'd never heard of. We went there to pore, goggle-eyed, over copies of *transition* and *Minotaure* and to spell our way through volumes of poems by Peret and Aragon. We went there for the delight of Gino's urbane conversation. In fact, about the only thing we didn't go there for was to buy books.

One or two local politicians had had the dotty idea that it would impress the electorate if they set themselves up as men of taste and they would sometimes drop in at the Leonardo. So would Melbourne's solitary press lordling. So would a handful of well-heeled 'professional men'. I hope they, at least, bought some things from time to time and, if they did, I hope Gino upped his prices. The rest of us were far too broke to think of buying the sumptuous goods he had to offer. We were strictly Penguin Books men. Gino never seemed to mind. I always had the impression that we were, if anything, rather more welcome than the paying customers.

Come to think of it, I did once buy a book from Gino- a lavish limited edition of a story by Richard Aldington printed at Nancy Cunard's Hours Press. Gino hunched his shoulders miserably and groaned a bit when I asked the price, as if the mention of money occasioned him deep physical pain, which quite possibly it did. Finally, he named some absurdly low figure and then, evidently deciding that it was nonetheless too much, insisted on throwing in another Hours Press production, Samuel Beckett's first published work, the poem *Whoroscope.*

Long afterwards, meeting Beckett in Paris, I mentioned that I had this booklet of his and told him where and how I'd acquired it. Beckett being Beckett, I suppose I shouldn't have been surprised at the effect which the innocuous little anecdote had on him. That furrowed anguished face of his grew still more furrowed, still more anguished. He evinced signs of consternation, of positive alarm. *Whoroscope* consisted of a single folded sheet enclosed in a flimsy cardboard cover, the sort of thing that is easily lost or casually thrown away, especially when the author, as was Beckett's case when the thing was published, is completely unknown. A large proportion of the tiny original edition must long since have disappeared. So how, asked Beckett, in a sort of panic, could one of the few survivors ever have got to Melbourne, of all places? There was, he insisted, something downright spooky about it. He himself hadn't seen a copy in twenty years.

For a moment, I was tempted to show myself as princely as Gino had been and to make Beckett a present of *Whoroscope*. Only for a moment, though, and, in due course, when my financial situation was sicklier than usual, I sold it for enough to keep me going for a couple of months. It was somehow altogether natural that Gino's friendly paw should have been extended like this, disregarding time and space, just when I needed it. There was always a touch of the necromancer about him.

Half the literary memoirs of the Twenties and Thirties contain some dewy-eyed recollections of those bookshops which were something more than merely commercial establishments where books are sold Sylvia Beach's Shakespeare and Co. in Paris, Harold Monro's Poetry Bookshop in London, Orioli's Lungarno in Florence. No doubt they were everything we've been told. But it seems unjust that a few of the rose petals scattered over them couldn't have been set aside for the Leonardo. If it had been located anywhere except in Melbourne it would have topped the list.

The Leonardo didn't even look like a bookshop. It looked like a rather untidy club. There was no counter, any more than there would be in a club. In the middle of the room there was a large table which, in a proper club, would have been bestrewn with copies of *Country Life* and the *Army List*. Here, such hearty literature had been replaced by those unwholesome *transitions* and *Minotaures* which awed us so deeply. Gino sat behind a smaller table in the corner. He was somewhat below average in height and distinctly above average in bulk. Years of unrestrained gobbling of pasta and risotto had given him an impressive belly and a round jowly face. With his head bent over a book or a portfolio of prints, as it invariably was, he looked, if such a thing can be imagined, like an Italianate Buddha meditating under the Bo Tree. Strangers were received with a polite but abstracted nod. For friends and acquaintances he would heave himself out of his chair and advance to shake hands in the European manner.

He must have been in Australia for ten years or more when I first knew him but he still retained a succulent *al dente* Italian accent. Sometimes, too, he would bring out a word into which he had introduced a slight and pleasing variation, not exactly Italian but rather pure Ginoan. To this day, for example, I can clearly hear his engaging pronunciation of 'sword', with no nonsense about eliding the 'w'. Sword, in Gino's mouth, was always flatly 'sward'.

In spite of these minor indiosyncrasies, his vocabulary was notable for its range and precision. If the exact word he wanted momentarily eluded him, he would interrupt himself for as long as was needed in order to recapture it. When he did recall it, it unfailingly proved well worth waiting for. In an article about him which I read not long ago, Desmond O'Grady describes one such moment and avers that it occurred during a public lecture. I could have sworn that it was in the course of a conversation with a small group of us at the Leonardo. Not that it matters. O'Grady and I both have a memory of Gino discoursing fluently on some sculpture or other. All of a sudden-silence, right in the middle of a sentence. It was as though poor Gino had had a stroke. One never quite got used to these abrupt spasms of speechlessness. Nothing was to be heard but little gasps and grunts of frustration. His hands clawed tormentedly in the air in an effort to trace the shapes he had in mind. We did our best to help him out.

'Spiral, Gino?'

'No, no, is not spiral.'

More cabbalistic scrabblings. 'Coiled?'

'No, no, no.'

One of us tried a long shot 'Convoluted?'

'No, no, no' and then, exhaling with the vast relief of a man who has at last succeeded in dislodging a fishbone in his throat, 'Helicoidal!' We felt like applauding.

With no swards to worry about and with plenty of time to pick his way among the convolutions and helicoidals, Gino's written English flowed smoothly. His style, however, remained unequivocally his own, and a splendidly rococo style it was. I seem to have preserved an article he published on El Greco and it abounds in characteristic Ginoan locutions. 'He digested the fire and projected it with the same craving incandescence in his own direction ... phosphorescence wriggling along edges of contours ... climaxes of well interwoven dramas, without the auxilium of preliminary tests ... '

Myself, though, I preferred Gino's prose as exemplified in his private correspondence. One particular letter I had from him has never ceased to enchant me. It was written from Rome, towards the end of Holy Week. As a stout anticlerical of the old school, Gino thought it desirable to warn me against visiting the city while the attendant ceremonies were going on. 'The streets,' he wrote, 'are full of singing religious displaying the utmost zeal. It is truly dismaying.'

Did he, I often wondered, find Australia equally dismaying? He admitted to a sense of nostalgia whenever he was away from it but in private he would also admit that the place now and again surprised him. I don't doubt it. Setting aside pasta and risotto, Gino's solitary enthusiasm was for the arts, and in Australia, in his day, that could be a suicidal taste. No singing religious ever displayed more zeal than the Australian authorities when it came to looking after the moral well-being of their little chicks. For them, every week was Holy Week. I don't say they would have gone so far as to nail an offender's ears to the church door but it's quite on the cards that they had a pillory tucked away somewhere for use in an emergency. Writers wrote and painters painted at their peril and, as Gino was to find out, booksellers led a pretty risky life, too.

Which particular official was responsible for choosing our reading matter for us? A mystery. I have an idea it was the Postmaster-General but it may just as easily have been the Minister for Agriculture, or the Chairman of the State Railways, or the Secretary of the Wharf Labourers' Union. After all, the view was, *anyone* can recognise dirt when it's shoved under his nose. Whoever he may have been - Minister, Chairman or Secretary - he stood out from the mass of politico - did know, it was that books were made for banning and he was the man to ban them. It goes without saying that he outlawed *Ulysses* and *Lady Chatterley's Lover* but he didn't overlook Beardsley's *Under the Hill* or George Moore's

Storyteller's Holiday or Aldous Huxley's *Brave New World* or the *Satyricon* or Ovid's *Metamorphoses*. And of course he sniffed long and hard at anything in French, whether it was *Le Roi Pausol* or Bossuet's funeral orations. Gino was really sticking his neck out by having those Aragons and Perets on his shelves. If you'd wanted to build up a fine library back then, you could have dispensed with those lists of The Hundred Best Books or The World's Great Masterpieces. A list of The Best Books Banned in Australia would have given you all the guidance you needed. The catch was that you couldn't have discovered what books were, in fact, banned. We weren't allowed, the point is, to know what it was that we weren't allowed to read. The only way of finding out was to try and buy this or that book and be told that you couldn't. My recollection is (unless perhaps I'm having an opium dream) that it was an offence in itself to possess a copy of the Commonwealth's *Index Librorum Prohibitorum*. I suppose the idea was that we might become overexcited merely by seeing the titles spelt out.

Gino's little bit of trouble, as it happens, had nothing to do with the books he stocked, even if they were in languages suspected of loitering with intent to commit a felony. Where he made his mistake was in consorting with Renoir. Innocent Gino had taken it into his head to enliven Leonardo's window with a reproduction of a Renoir nude, breasts and all. Our bureaucratic nannies had never been able to take breasts, so to speak, in their stride. They once clamped down on a book of Norman Lindsay's because the jacket depicted a lady with *one* bare breast. The Renoir reproduction, with two, had them deary-meing and goodness-graciousing and what-nexting as if they'd been brought fact to face with the Kama Sutra. Prompt and energetic action was called for. And taken. Gino had scarcely placed the Renoir in his window when, with a cop watching his every move, he was taking it out again.

I would have given a lot to see Gino's face on learning that Renoir was a misdemeanour. And I would have liked to be around, too, when he was prevented in the nick of time from turning us all into rapists by importing some Modigliani reproductions. I wonder if he ever realised how lucky he was as a second offender, almost an habitual criminal, not to be manacled and carted off to clink.

That was what happened to Robert Close when he published his novel, *Love Me, Sailor*. The nannies were in a terrible state. They'd been so sure, the dear old things, that no-one could be dirtier than Renoir, except perhaps Modigliani, and here was Close, worse than either. Whether the nannies had ever considered trying to extradite Renoir and Modigliani to face trial I couldn't say although it wouldn't surprise me if they had, but putting Close in the dock presented no such problem. He was right to hand, waiting to be nabbed. And nabbed he was, hauled before the court on a charge of obscenity, found guilty (what else?) and refused bail. The judge wanted to spend a leisurely weekend deciding just how tough a sentence he could pronounce. Meantime, Close was handcuffed (presumably to make sure that he didn't start writing another book) and borne off to prison in the Black Maria. 'A man who is responsible for this work,' observed the judge in a giant eructation of forensic reasoning, 'cannot quibble if he is sent to gaol.' Gino would have admired the happy choice of the word 'quibble'.

Judges have to endure their little disappointments like the rest of us and it must have caused quite a pang to His Lordship when he realised that the maximum penalty he could impose was a lousy three months. And I don't doubt that his golf game went all to hell when a higher court reduced the penalty to a mere fine. One can only hope that he was slightly consoled when Close announced that he had had enough of Australia's prissy view of life (not to mention its ready use of handcuffs) and would henceforward live abroad. So there was that much gained. One writer less.

I didn't know Close well but we'd met occasionally in Melbourne and I recall being struck by a mildness of manner which was, to say the least, unexpected in a man who'd sailed before the mast for some years and whose life had been a hard one even after he left the sea. That was before the hullabaloo over *Love Me, Sailor.* Later we had a drink together when he came to France (where his book was published without any significant increase in sex crimes) and he had changed very considerably. He was an angry man. There was nothing remotely mild about his remarks on his own experience and on the Australian attitude towards artists in general. God knows what would have happened to him if the judge and the Crown Prosecutor had overheard his conversation. They would have clapped the darbies on his wrists in a flash.

If Ionesco thought he'd invented the theatre of the absurd he was much mistaken. Australia's courts were miles ahead of him. Especially in the obscenity trials (and there were plenty of them going on at that time), judges and learned counsel and witnesses for the prosecution regularly made themselves into stupendous figures of fun. Close's trial was different. The clowns had turned nasty. There wasn't a laugh in the whole performance.

When Max Harris had his run-in with the law it was good clean family entertainment from start to finish. To begin with, Max always had a romantic and rather touching love of publicity. During his trial, he did a good deal of magniloquent snorting about freedom of speech and artistic integrity and the insanity of censorship (and of course he was absolutely right). But nobody is ever going to persuade me that he didn't enjoy himself one hundred per cent. Besides, there was never any danger of his being shoved into a cell and, finally, the chief witness for the prosecution revealed himself to be one of the most hilarious slapstick artists of the day.

The poems responsible for Max's ordeal (although, as I say, I'm willing to bet that it was no ordeal to Max) were the work of the ersatz poet Em Malley. They were about as sexually arousing as *Hymns Ancient and Modern* but when Max published them in his *Angry Penguins* magazine they gave a terrible jolt to at least one reader. Detective Vogelsang could see depravity that was hidden from everyone else. You couldn't, as he himself would probably have put it, pull the wool over his eyes.

A detective who appeared in another obscenity case readily acknowledged, when asked if he was familiar with Shelley, that he had indeed come across someone of that name, a bloke who lived in Woolloomooloo. In the matter of Lord Byron he wasn't so sure. On the spur of the moment, he confessed with a manly frankness which well became him, he couldn't recollect whether Lord Byron had been on Admiral Mountbatten's staff during the war or not.

These two crime-busters may have been one and the same, but if they weren't, it ought to be recorded that Detective Vogelsang hadn't got a thing to learn from his colleague when it came to knockabout comedy. One of Ern's poems, for instance, was set in a park, a park at night, and the detective was on to the significance of that like a shot. 'I have found,' he said, 'that people who go into parks at night go there for an immoral purpose.' Fair-minded though, he conceded that possibly 'my experience as a police officer might tinge my appreciation of poetry'. Who would have thought that judges and cops had such a delicate feeling for words? 'Tinge', 'quibble' - I'm not sure that Flaubert could have done any better. And how about the sort of verbal sixth sense which enabled the detective to affirm that while he didn't know what 'incestuous' actually *meant*, it had an unmistakable whiff of indecency about it?

I hate to think of Detective Vogelsang and his peers being forgotten. They gave so much pleasure to so many people. When will some sedulous anthologist come along and produce a monumental *sottisier* to preserve their solemn inanities? It mightn't be a bad idea at the same time, I must admit, to envisage a second volume of excerpts from the literature some of us were turning out at that time. In our own way, we *avant-garde* sophisticates could, and now and again did, show ourselves right up there in the same class as Detective Vogelsang when it came to inanity.

Australian bookshops used to be overloaded with imported literature, no argument about that. Not any more. What hits you now is the Shenandoah-like flow of remorselessly nationalistic compilations *Historic Australian Shearing Sheds, The Bumper Book of Australian Cock-roaches, Everybody's Album of Australian Barbed-Wire Fences, Whither Australian Bottle Tops*? Go into an Australian bookshop nowadays and you may not find the book you're looking for but you're certainly left in no doubt as to what country you're in.

It's extraordinary that nobody so far has undertaken what I'm confident would be a runaway best-seller - *The Australian Treasury of Unabashed Cretinisms*.

Max Harris in 1943.

TWO

The war had brought the American poet Karl Shapiro to Australia with the US Army. There he was in Melbourne and not finding it any too easy to cope, by the sound of it. He was daunted by the 'bungalows with the lace aprons, and the children crying out for autographs, and' (but this must have been the good old divine afflatus at work) 'the moonlight and the sheep'. Altogether, he was in a hell of a state. What s ems to have saved him was that, mooching glumly around the place, he chanced on Gino's Leonardo shop. It must have been the Leonardo I can't believe that there was anywhere else where he could have picked up a copy of *Comment*, the only 'modernist' magazine for as far as the eye could see. Anyway, pick it up he did and the discovery, he wrote to Cecily Crozier who edited it, was 'a shot in the arm of a dying, fainting, failing Yank'.

Comment (later on it became *A Comment*) had given an invigorating shot to a number of arms besides Shapiro's. We - meaning, among others, James Gleeson, Adrian Lawlor, Max Harris, Michael Kean and Muir Holburn - were a frustrated bunch. No editor had ever approached us humbly - or in any other frame of mind, for that matter - asking us to let him publish something we'd written. If there was any consolation it was that we had never received a rejection slip - there was no-one to reject us. We couldn't help envying the painters when we compared their situation to ours. They had no trouble communicating with the outside world, the world, that is, outside Gino's bookshop and the Petrushka Cafe. If nothing else offered, they could always invite potential buyers to visit their studios and look around. This was accepted practice, even for the top men in the profession, the kind who could name their own price for painting you a picture of gumtrees or bullock teams. Then there were the group shows - 'Artists Against Fascism', 'Artists for Civil Liberties', 'Contemporary Symbolism', 'New Orientations', that sort of thing. Luck had to be really running against you if you couldn't get a canvas into one or another of these.

With a touch of imagination, too, you could devise your own cunning solution to the problem of getting your message across. Sidney Nolan, early in his career, had the cute idea of displaying his work in a bicycle shop, I think it was, or an ironmongery or something. Nobody thought any the worse of him. On the contrary. It was widely felt that he'd struck a blow for democracy by bringing art to the people. It's true that he didn't succeed in bringing the people to art since practically no-one turned up but nevertheless he'd held an exhibition, he'd communicated, which was a damn sight more than we could do.

Maybe if we'd hunted around for long enough we would eventually have dug up an ironmonger to let us intone our compositions on his premises. But I don't somehow think so my guess is that Sid had cornered the only aesthetically-inclined ironmonger in the city. Besides, a recital among the frying pans and half-inch nails wouldn't have been such a great improvement on our usual makeshift technique of simply grabbing hold of any old mate who happened to pass by and reading at him whenever we'd produced something that struck us as more than ordinarily good. The plain truth is that there was only one way to bring the roses to our cheeks, and that was to give us *print*.

Of course, there was a scattering of 'little magazines' in the country - roughly one to every quarter of a million square miles, according to my estimate - but they weren't for the likes of us. Every last one of them was committed to some loony creed or other. We wouldn't have stood a chance, for example, of getting into any of the communist publications. These were run by very grumpy fellows indeed. Their attitude towards what they described as 'bourgeois experimentalism' was censorious and if there was one thing we were keen on it was being experimental. The communists wouldn't consider anything that wasn't rugged, forthright, straight-from-the-shoulder and suitable for reading by the masses in the intervals of being ground down.

The university reviews weren't quite so dour but they in general prescribed a left-liberal line which had to be toed by contributors, and while most of us (but not I, to my lasting shame) were leftish in our views, we had an aversion to lines being traced for our fidgety feet. That left the billabong-happy nationalistic magazines but in order to be accepted by these you had to have a good working knowledge of the Arunta dialect and to feel a tug at your heart whenever you glimpsed a wombat.

Very occasionally, some temerarious fantast would bring out a magazine with no ambition except to publish writing which was a trifle more sprightly than the stock exchange reports in the evening paper. Cyril Pearl's *Stream* was an outstanding example. But how long did *Stream* hang on? It was before my time but I have an idea it was for no more than two or three issues. That was what was so dispiriting about such ventures as *Stream* the death throes practically coincided with the birth pangs. If you didn't manage to get something into the first number you were probably already too late to get it in at all.

When Peter Bellew took over as editor of *Art in Australia*, it looked for a moment as if we were going to have a little magazine that was a big mazagine. The old *Art in Aust-*

ralia had been a very prim production. *Art in Australia,* as *Art in Australia* saw it, consisted of publishing as many reproductions of Hans Heysen and Sir Arthur Streeton as its readers could consume without getting the shakes. The accompanying texts had all the irrepressible gaiety of a tract designed for distribution at a meeting of the Plymouth Brethren.

One crack from Bellew's whip and the drowsy old thing was turning cartwheels. Nobody knew better than Bellew who was who and what was what in the arts and, with the bountiful backing of Warwick Fairfax, he could let himself go. I doubt if Sir Arthur Streeton ever got a look-in again. The most outrageous names began to appear among the contributors - Herbert Read and Andre Breton and, if I'm not mistaken, Salvador Dali and a whole bundle of exotics who had us open-mouthed and wide-eyed. And to cap it all, as if their arrival in our midst wasn't already enough, we nobodies were permitted, in fact we were encouraged, to hobnob with our betters, to see our names in print side-by-side with theirs, our cheeks by their jowls. Albert Tucker was one of the local boys to make good in this way, I think, Adrian Lawlor certainly was. I actually wriggled in myself and since I was only about eighteen at the time I was so intoxicated by what had happened to me that I remained drunk and more or less disorderly for the following twelve months. Forty years on (no, fifty, heaven help me) I can still recapture something of my juvenile exultation.

With a sponsor as lavish as Fairfax and an editor as discerning as Bellew (who, if I myself didn't have anything to offer him just when he wanted it, could always fill in with an essay by Clive Bell or a poem by W. H. Auden), there was every reason in the world to assume that *Art in Australia* was there for keeps. The trouble was that magazines, however liberally subsidised, need a minimum readership and the readers of Australian magazines devoted to the arts tended to consist almost exclusively of their contributors. So, in due course, *Art in Australia* gave a pathetic little sigh, fell back on the pillows and was buried to the noise of the mourning of a mighty nation - well, call it one-tenth of one per cent of a mighty nation.

Such was the dispiriting atmosphere prevailing when Cecily Crozier took it into her head to launch her *Comment*. She must have been raving mad. I've been delicately hinting that there was never a good moment at which to start a highbrow magazine but Cecily chose the very worst. As Karl Shapiro was to find out, there was a war on, and in wartime it seems to be generally agreed that there's something unpatriotic, something downright subversive, about any cultural activity other than painting portraits of generals or writing dispatches as a war correspondent. To her credit, Cecily didn't give a hoot for whatever tut-tutting disapproval she may have encountered but she must have felt tempted on occasion to call the whole harebrained enterprise off when she came up against the material difficulties involved. For another wartime phenomenon is that, within minutes of hostilities breaking out, everything, from bootlaces to wheelbarrows, and everybody, from circus acrobats to monumental masons, virtually disappear overnight. When *Comment* came into existence there was a shortage of printers and a shortage of type, a shortage of staples, a shortage, for all I know, of ink.

And, first and foremost, there was a shortage of paper. That was needed for hortatory posters telling us to keep our traps shut in case the enemy was listening, for pamphlets instructing housewives how to camouflage their front porches, and for Top Secret reports on improved techniques for digging trenches. What was left for *Comment* was wrapping paper, blotting paper, lavatory paper and whatever other scraps the dauntless Cecily could wrench from the reluctant claws of the rationing authorities. It certainly doesn't do any harm for an avant-garde magazine to look out of the ordinary but *Comment* looked rather more out of the ordinary than most.

Paper aside, the first number conformed pretty much to the rules, that's to say there were some listless linocuts, which were all the go back then, and very few capital letters (no *avant-garde* magazine was really avant unless it displayed a marked preference for the lower case). The actual contents were something of a letdown. There was a note by Cecily on a forthcoming show of paintings by her uncle, Frank Crozier, which only went to show that her heart was in the right place because Uncle Frank was not by any means 'modern'. As a matter of fact, that first number was almost entirely consanguineous. There was some cryptic symbolical prose by Irvine Green who I fancy was Cecily's husband then; and there were some worrying snippets of verse by Sylvia Green who I take it was some kind of a relation of Irvine's. The cost of this family album was sixpence.

I never elucidated the mystery of why Cecily decided to toss her firecracker magazine into the yawning face of the Australian public. She had never had any experience (if *Comment* proved anything, it proved that) and indeed at one point she furnished an editorial which specifically stated that there was no editor. Nor was she looking for an opportunity to publish her own works. Apart from that self-effacing disclaimer, the kindly tribute to Uncle Frank and a preliminary statement of 'aims', I don't believe she ever put in an appearance in the magazine. It's true that she had always, as they say, been interested in the arts but the closest she had

Adrian Lawlor.

ever come to practising them was when she worked for a while in London as an artist's model. Besides, hordes of people are interested in the arts - or claim to be - but remarkably few of them show any inclination to spend their time and energy, let alone their money, running magazines for which there is no noticeable demand.

It's possible that Cecily's eccentric decision to start a cultural magazine had something to do with her cosmopolitan background. She was born in Australia but between the ages of ten and seventeen had lived in the South of France - and you could learn a lot in the South of France at seventeen. She spent the next six years in London, followed by two years in Alexandria where you could learn even more than in the South of France. These were the days when an Australian who had visited New Zealand was looked on with awe as having made the Grand Tour. Anyone who got as far as Fiji qualified as a seasoned globe-trotter. We didn't let on, of course, but we were immensely impressed by Cecily's gallivantings around the world.

She must have got quite a jolt when she finally returned to Australian in 1938. It wasn't the South of France by a long chalk and it certainly wasn't Alexandria. Only a few months earlier, Sir Robert Menzies (who, as Federal Attorney-General, was well placed to know what art was permissible and what art deserved to be locked up) had devised a plan to create a 'Royal Australian Academy'. The only outcome of this brainwave was that it inspired Adrian Lawlor to write his uproarious lampoon *Arquebus* but the mere fact that such a loony project could be put forward provides a dismal indication of the state of affairs in Australia's 'art world' at that time.

The same *Arquebus* offers a pointer to the no less dismal

situation confronting Australian writers then. Here was a wonderfully murderous piece of satire, as good as Wyndham Lewis at his best and immeasurably better than Whistler with his Gentle Art. I've tried it on people who knew nothing of Australia and its artistic ups and downs, people who had never even heard, incredible as it seems, of Sir Robert Menzies, and who were instantaneously captivated by its wit, its sublime zaniness, its gleefully adroit hanging, drawing and quartering of Sir Robert and his followers. Adrian published it - at his own expense, naturally - and it aroused about as much enthusiasm as a reprint of *Foxe's Book of Martyrs*. It fetches substantial prices now, I see from the booksellers' catalogues. What I remember are the piles of unwrapped copies, straight from the printers, which for years were stacked up in Adrian's studio. Nobody wanted them even as a gift.

That being the way things were, Cecily, as I say, may have felt that she had to do something to avoid succumbing to the country's endemic narcolepsy. There's some evidence for this in the brief note which appeared in the first number of *Comment*. 'Our aim is stimulation,' it proclaimed with what sounds to me like a note of desperation, and it went on to voice the hope that 'we will extract from the surrounding gloom a few people who will be really interested in our effort to put into print the newest ideas in writing and design.'

The newest ideas turned out to be positively decrepit on occasion experimentalism in the arts always runs the risk of swallowing its own tail. Especially at the beginning, *Comment* published a suffocating amount of ouija board poetry and planchette prose, palsied imitations of the surrealists mostly. Cecily's aim may have been stimulation but there's no denying that some of her contributors were as stimulating as tsetse flies and were not much more gifted as practitioners of the arts.

On the other hand, it's equally undeniable that Cecily, while she may have put into print some stupefyingly fatuous claptrap, did nonetheless give a number of authentic writers an opportunity to say their piece at a time when they would have found it hard to get a word in edgewise anywhere else. Max Harris, in particular, was one of her favourites, and rightly. His poems were glitteringly accomplished, he produced some spirited (and sometimes staggeringly wrong-headed) criticism, and his novel, *The Vegetative Eye*, although I couldn't admire it as much as Max did, didn't by any means merit the roughing-up he received from A. D. Hope in a celebrated review.

The surrealist artist James Gleeson was another of Cecily's star contributors. His poems left me cold, indeed they came close to giving the impression that this was the whole idea, that the reader was to be frozen out. His prose was a very different matter. He wrote as few painters have done (and few writers, come to that) with such distinction that any proper God-fearing editor would have rejected him without hesitation. In spite of my real admiration for his work, however, and although I had no reason whatever to dislike him (we had never even met), I took a heavy-handed swipe at him in a rather inept squib and have felt remorseful about it ever since.

Some boisterous battles were waged in the pages of *Comment.* The exuberant Max Harris, who in those days had a pronounced distaste for peace and quiet, opened hostilities by hoeing into Adrian Lawlor. This nearly led to a formal severing of diplomatic relations between Max and me since, apart from my profound personal affection for Adrian, I had already reached the conclusion that no such obstreperous genius had ever erupted in Australia. His satire had a *kukri* edge to it and with one dextrous sweep he spatchcocked Max who thereafter preferred to devote himself to bedevilling another old friend of mine in the person of P. R. Stephensen. Adrian, for his part, wiped the blood from his blade and turned on Michael Keon, yet another friend, who had a considerable polemical gift of his own.

Myself, I got off pretty lightly on the whole. I was mildly chided by Muir Holburn when I published a blustering anathema directed at every category of Australian society I could think of and, as provocatively as I could manage, contending (a not too original thesis) that 'the artist' was a natural aristocrat who loomed gigantically over the riffraff. It was an adolescent piece of arrogance and Muir Holburn could reasonably have trounced me a good deal harder than he did. A Mr Smith made up for Holburn's mansuetude. Mr Smith spent his time, I gathered, hunting for fascists like an old lady peering under the bed for burglars. My light-hearted outburst apparently persuaded him that at last his apprehensions had been justified and he hurried to tell the neighbours all about it. I (and, for what they call good measure, Adrian) had scared the life out of him ('Oh dear, my palpitations!'). There had been a fascist under the bed, two of them, in fact, Adrian and me. I can't assert it with certainty because I don't have the charge sheet to consult, but I rather think that Mr Smith spread the word that I was in the pay of Dr Goebbels.

I hadn't even known that Dr Goebbels was in the market for my kind of stuff but Mr Smith was a communist and I was familiar with the communists' habit of identifying anyone they disliked with the inner circle at Berchtesgaden. Mr Smith's squawk of alarm accordingly came as no surprise to me. Adrian, on the other hand, who had only the barest nodding acquaintance with the everyday world, was dreadfully puzzled.

'What is a fascist, Alister? I've often wondered.'

'Well, really, Adrian, I thought Mr Smith had made that clear. A fascist is someone who doesn't know what a fascist is. You see where that leaves you?'

'No, I don't - that's the problem. Where does it leave me? Has it left me? Or have I left it? These are troubling questions. And wilt it leave me thus - whoever or whatever "it" may be - say nay, say nay, for shame. Besides, Goebbels? That's a suburb of Glasgow, surely?'

'No, no, the suburb is the Gorbals. Goebbels lives somewhere in Germany, or so I've always understood.'

'Ah, that makes everything much clearer. I couldn't understand why you'd be in the pay of Glasgow ... '

Albert Tucker gave Mr Smith a thwack which may have been mortal - at least, I've never heard of him since. All I had to do, therefore, was to sit back and go on drawing my weekly wages from Dr Goebbels.

I never saw any sign that Cecily was especially fascinated by the things she published in *Comment*. Conceivably, she didn't read them. But she was addicted to the company of writers and artists and whenever we chose to drop in on her we were received with an enthusiasm which we didn't always encounter. She lived in a small suburban house which seemed an incongruous setting for someone editing a rumbustiously modern magazine but it was nice to be made welcome. Cecily would serve vast bowls of spaghetti and allow us, with unwavering patience, to bawl and dispute and recite. Conceivably, once again, she didn't listen to us but if she was actually thinking all the time about something else she concealed the fact perfectly and we were able to put on our little performances in the conviction that we had a really appreciative audience.

The pubs would have been closed for hours by the time we left Cecily in peace and we still had plenty to say. There was nothing left for us to do but walk endlessly through the empty streets at two a.m., now and again stopping to squat on the kerbside. For a change of scenery we might trudge through one of the parks. It was just as well Detective Vogelsang never caught us but, whatever his experience as a policeman might have taught him, we were there for no more immoral purpose than arguing about Spender or Day Lewis. We would much sooner have been sitting around a marble-topped table in a Paris cafe or in a cafe anywhere else.

I was touched on reading an article of Michael Keon's not long ago to find him reminiscing about one of these nocturnal hikes of ours, in the course of which he asserts that I recited Richard Aldington's *A Dream in the Luxembourg* from memory in what he describes with friendly mockery as my 'ex cathedra voice'. *A Dream in the Luxembourg* is a very long poem. To recite it in full would take at least an hour. If Michael is telling the truth I brought off a singular feat. I wish I possessed the same superlative memory now. It would make the writing of these random recollections considerably easier.

I've been figuring it out and I see that I took an inordinately sunny view of affairs when I suggested that one-tenth of one per cent of the population might have taken a genuine interest in a cultural magazine. The population of Australia in the Forties must have been somewhere in the region of ten million. One-tenth of one per cent of that is ten thousand. *Comment,* after it had been in existence for some years, achieved a readership of 300. Cecily appealed for an extra 150 subscribers (at about a dollar a year) in order to keep going. She never got them.

That was the end of *Comment*. It had been a brave effort. With very little money to spend on it, with the countless material problems confronting her all the time, Cecily had fought the good fight for seven long years - *Comment* outlasted Cyril Connolly's *Hori on* which had a millionaire backing it. Cecily announced the demise of her magazine with pardonable melancholy but without rancour. In her place I would have been inclined to catch the next boat back to Alexandria. She simply withdrew from the literary world, such as it was, and applied herself to the breeding of dachshunds. They were probably just as addicted to literature as the rest of the population.

Cecily Crozier, as seen in *Comment*.

THREE

Periodically, Max Harris would catapult himself from his Adelaide fief over to Melbourne. His arrival invariably set lights flashing. The young Max gave the impression of being perpetually under the influence of some prepotent stimulant. His energy was paranormal. He could be in twenty different places at once doing something different in each. Poems and articles came rocketing out of him with dizzying velocity. He had an immense circle of friends and acquaintances and could converse volubly with them throughout whole nights and show no signs of fatigue at the end. He had evidently found time to read everything published since Caxton. On top of all this, he bafflingly continued to edit his *Angry Penguins* magazine.

Angry Penguins came into existence almost simultaneously with the launching of *Comment* so that out of the blue we suddenly had two magazines where ten minutes earlier there hadn't been any. The name which Max had selected for his publication was taken, to the surprise of no-one who knew him, from one of his poems and, myself, I always thought it mildly absurd. In every other respect, however, *Angry Penguins* made poor little *Comment* look distinctly amateurish. It didn't ban the use of capital letters. It was blessedly free of those lackadaisical linocuts to which Cecily was so attached. It was printed (heaven knows how Max managed this) on paper that bore some resemblance to paper meant to be printed on. Finally, it published a lot of people whom Cecily had overlooked or who, which is more probable, had decided that *Comment* wasn't for them. Gino appeared in both but Geoffrey Dutton, an angry penguin from start to finish, only once contributed to *Comment* - and then his name was misspelled. The charming and greatly gifted composer Dorian Le Gallienne wrote for *Angry Penguins* but never for *Comment*. So too did Albert Tucker, a man of restless and impassioned intelligence and a natural writer as well as the consummate painter everyone now recognises. Max's talents included an astonishingly mature judgment, there's no denying.

It was plentifully denied at the time of the Em Malley hoax. The 'anti-modernists' (of which there was a considerable surplus) exulted that Max had fallen flat on his face. It's a dusty old story which those who were around while the business was going on have surely forgotten and which a younger generation has surely never heard of. What happened was that two traditionalist poets (and not bad, either), Harold Stewart and James McAuley, assembled chunks from books, technical reports, advertisements and anything else lying around the house, stirred them around a bit, chopped them into unequal lines, garnished them with some phrases of their own, and submitted the resultant Irish stew to Max as the work of an unknown poet called Ern Malley. Max was instantaneously captivated and published the entire collection, prefaced by an incautious eulogy, in a 'Special Em Malley' number of *Angry Penguins*, whereupon the two triumphant pranksters revealed what they'd been up to.

This must be the oldest literary tease in the world but for some reason the newspapers leapt at it and the population was in stitches. What the boys on the Stock Exchange saw in the Ern Malley joke was not a guying of one individual 'school' of poets (which is fair enough, whoever the butts may be) but a guying of all poets and all poetry. That was what had them slapping their thighs on this occasion. Max stuck to it that Stewart and McAuley, whatever they may have intended, had produced poems of the highest merit. The rest of the *Angry Penguins* crowd, or most of them, went along with Max. Sir Herbert Read, no less, weighed in with a letter to the effect that he himself considered Em to be a genuine poet. But even Sir Herbert couldn't do much to help. *Angry Penguins* continued to appear for another year or two but the hoax had been a custard pie right in the kisser.

I hate having to come clean but I joined in the guffawing myself. I should have remembered that if you find yourself on the same side as the burgesses you must be wrong. *Mea culpa*. The poems I jeered at I can now see are indeed of a weird and moving beauty. I haven't read them in years but whole fragments, I discover, have stayed with me and constantly resurface in my memory - a primitive test but for me a conclusive one. Max was quite right. Ern Malley was a poet superior to Stewart and McAuley put together.

Just recently, a friend sent me a piece by Max recalling the *Angry Penguins* era. He and all of us, he records, were frankly looking for trouble. We got it. What Max calls the gumtree school was scandalised by our breakaway from bush-balladry, the Stewarts and McAuleys deplored our deviation from 'traditional values', that man who's always somewhere in the street was either unaware of our existence or thought we were barmy, the decent chaps saw us as a threat to Church and State, and the communists, of course, as Bert Tucker pointed out in his deft evisceration of Mr Smith, took exactly the same view as the fascist bogeymen in the matter of decadent art. Nobody loved us. It was wonderful.

Max usually got in touch whenever he came to Melbourne. We headed for the nearest pub, naturally...

The Australian pubs of fifty years ago are worth a digression. They were the closest thing to lazar-houses since the Middle Ages. You took your life in your hands whenever you ordered a beer. It was good beer but the way it was served was something you had to get accustomed to. I doubt if anyone ever had the nerve to ask for a clean glass. You might just as well have worn a green carnation in your buttonhole and be done with it. You got the glass used by the previous drinker, the stale suds still clinging to its sides. As a concession to customers' finicky prejudices, it might be dipped briefly into a dank tarn of cold water before being refilled but that was the most you could expect. I'll never know why we didn't all go down with Tapanuli fever or the black Formosa corruption.

Towards the end of the day came the really ghoulish part. Pubs closed at six sharp. The wage-slaves emerged from offices and factories at five. That gave them one hour in which to slake thirsts that took a lot of slaking. By ten past five, a bawling concourse of single-minded citizens was lined up at the counter, seven, eight, nine deep. There was no more namby-pamby rinsing of glasses. Speed was what counted. Glasses were emptied in one stupendous gulp, passed over intervening heads to the bar, refilled and passed back. By ten to six, everyone was hoarse, good and drunk, and looking for a fight. That was the moment to make your getaway. If you were quick enough on your feet you might escape without somebody being sick over your shoes.

Changes have to be expected, I suppose, but when I returned to Australia for the first time in years I'm not ashamed to confess that I could have wept when I saw what was gone. Most of the dives I used to frequent had vanished altogether - Richardson's, the Four Courts, and a dozen others whose names I can't recall - and those that were left had completely lost their endearing old charms. There were tables and chairs (in my day it was illegal to sit down), clean floors, freshly painted walls, tempting counter lunches (you couldn't, when I was one-and twenty, get so much as a salted peanut). No sooner was a glass drunk from than it was shot into a contraption which sprayed it all over with a jet of steam. The germs of Tapanuli fever and the black Formosa corruption wouldn't have stood a chance. No six o'clock closing you could swig away until far into the night or rather (and this was the most distressing change to be observed) sip genteelly. No fights, no spewing. One might just as well have been in the Ritz. There was a lump in my throat and a tear in my eye as I contemplated the transformation that had taken place.

Like the others, the Mitre Tavern has been sadly smartened up. That was where Max and I did most of our drinking. There was a hitching post outside which made the Mitre an historical monument by our standards. It was also (although it was situated at the opposite end of the city from the minute Bohemian quarter) much frequented by artists. In particular, it was the meeting place of a William Morris look-alike called Justus Jorgensen whenever he and his followers came to town. Normally, the whole bunch huddled together in a community located in what they liked to think of as 'the bush', actually a not-so-very-outer outer suburb. They wore shaggy beards and had toil-worn hands because they never stopped building mock-medieval houses which were a damn sight more mock than medieval. In between times they painted highly respectable pictures in conformity with some theory which I never discovered. They disapproved wholeheartedly of people like Max and myself - 'modernists', radicals, who couldn't tell a merlon from a crenel. They knew us by sight and would glower malignantly at us from as far away as they could get. It was worth going to the Mitre just for that.

One day in 1943 Max turned up there with sensational news. He and John Reed, a solicitor with a rich wife and aesthetic leanings, had established a publishing firm, Reed & Harris, which proposed to publish books, of all things. I couldn't credit it. Books simply weren't published in Australia then, it wasn't done. A history of Government House or a guide to racing form might hit the stalls occasionally but that was about as far as it went. Anything else required the author to pay for the publication himself, usually under the imprint of some fictitious 'press'. My own choice, when I could no longer resist having a book to my name, was the Warlock Press, in pious memory of the composer Peter Warlock on whom I had a great crush at the time; Adrian's *Arquebus* appeared under the wonderfully inappropriate banner of the Ruskin Press; and so on.

What happened then depended on the author's particular temperament. The only certainty was that he wouldn't get his money back. You could distribute a few copies to friends and use the rest to light fires (which is what I did) or you could stack them up against the wall, like Adrian, and watch the silverfish having a treat. Or you could do as Frank Dalby Davison did with his admirable *Man-Shy* and hawk your stuff from door to door - my door among others, I remember. I bought a copy. I wonder how many he sold altogether.

In the Thirties, P. R. Stephensen had created his Endeavour Press - a genuine press, not a fictitious one - in an attempt to show that an Australian publishing house could turn out 'serious' books and still survive. Where did it get him? On the breadline, practically. He had as much energy and enthusiasm as Max and (which neither Max nor Reed could claim) he had had plenty of experience when running the Fanfrolico Press and the Mandrake Press in London some years previously. He had Norman Lindsay's practical backing and (no doubt Detective Vogelsang would reject the phrase as applied to Norman Lindsay) moral support. Financing was provided by the *Bulletin* which had much more money than John Reed. In spite of which, the Endeavour Press went gurgling down the drain and that was that.

Nothing of the kind was going to happen to Reed and Harris, Max assured me, and since I still looked incredulous, he came out with a clincher.

'We want to do a book of your poems, of course.'

'You want to do a book of my poems?'

'That's what I said.'

'I don't have to pay for it myself?'

'No, of course you don't.'

'Not even go halves?'

'I'm telling you, aren't I? Look, what do you say to an advance of ten quid?'

That was big money.

'You'll give me ten quid?'

'That's right.'

'You're not asking me to give it to you?'

'No, for Christ's sake. We're real publishers, don't you understand?'

Max had assumed his new role to perfection. He now, while I gawped at him, produced a cheque book. That convinced me. None of us had ever had cheque books. They belonged to a weird world which we'd never entered. Max had certainly never had one before. He tore out a form and filled it in with the negligent air of a man who'd spent his whole life cornering markets and effecting mergers. He handed it across. 'Pay to the order of Alister Kershaw the sum of Ten Pounds .. .' I couldn't doubt any longer.

With only a minimum of condescension, Max explained that I could endorse his cheque and cash it there and then over the bar. Sure enough, the Mitre gave me the money. When we eventually lurched out some hours later I'd given it all back to the Mitre. It was, after all, an occasion for celebration ...

Max was unlike most writers he had no spleen in his make-up. Nobody was readier to praise other people's work. He undoubtedly got a genuine kick out of getting his friends' books into print. His partner may have felt the same way as a rule. Not in my case though. The most perfect harmony prevailed between John Reed and myself. He disliked me as much as I disliked him.

I couldn't imagine how anyone could conceivably find anything to object to in me. But I was quite clear as to what I objected to in Reed. He came across as what the French call a *pisse-froid*. I never heard him laugh. He may have smiled once or twice but I doubt it, and certainly not when I was around. I would have remembered anything so out of character. Perhaps in company more congenial than mine he was a barrel of fun, constantly bubbling over with high spirits. Whenever I saw him he displayed all the joviality of an elder of the Presbyterian Church dealing with an unrepentant adulterer. He ejected his words between barely parted lips as if he were trying to spit as unobtrusively as possible. He was the only man I ever knew who could pronounce my name so that it sounded like a malediction.

On deciding to abandon soliciting in favour of the arts, he had turned his and his wife's home, 'Heidi', into a sort of cultural open house. It wasn't open to me, naturally, but Max and Bert Tucker and Arthur Boyd and Sid Nolan and various other friends and acquaintances were in fairly frequent attendance. Through them I had intermittent glimpses of life at 'Heidi'. They all thought very well of Reed and did their best to lead me to an appreciation of his sterling qualities. It was no good. Their descriptions of the internal set-up did nothing to win me over. It sounded like Jorgensen's medieval community turned on its head. From what I gathered, the aim was to achieve an amalgam of sophistication and the simple life, earnest conversations alternating with the philosophical milking of cows.

That book of mine to which Max had so impulsively committed the firm of Reed & Harris brought me into somewhat closer contact with Reed, although not with his wife, Sunday, who was reputed to be Reed's mentor in artistic matters, which may have been true, as well as his major source of financing, which was certainly true. I encountered her only once when, as a loyal spouse, she eyed me with visible reprehension and promptly left the room. However, she didn't veto publication of my book, which indicated a commendable ability to distinguish between art and the artist - an ability, it was rumoured, which she didn't consistently exercise.

My book was to be one of a series, the others being by Max's old buddy and mine, Geoffrey Dutton, and by the American poet, Harry Roskolenko, who, like Shapiro, had been cast up on our shores by the US Army. The three books, Reed announced, were to be 'uniform'. Like hell they were.

Either because of wartime restrictions or because he thought the idea would be daringly *avant-garde*, Reed had decided that the books would be printed on almost transparent paper doubled over to make it opaque. I'd had enough of peculiar paper with Cecily and said so. Reed promptly went fantee. I received a very cross letter indeed. 'Dear Alister,' and, so help me, a distinct smell of loathing rose from the typed salutation, 'you write with the petulance of a wounded prima donna.' I think he felt he'd coined a new and deadly phrase which would ensure that there'd be no more impudence from me. He was wrong.

I wasn't, in the next round of this ridiculous spat, merely guilty of impudence. I went on to outright blasphemy by saying I didn't care for Sid Nolan's design for the jacket and wouldn't have it at any price.

'And what, may I ask, do you take exception to?'

'I think it's shit.'

There was a murderous silence. When Reed had recovered sufficiently to be able to speak again, his 'Alister' sounded more than ever like a ritual curse with bell, book and candle.

'I'm afraid, *Alister*, that you have no eye for beauty.'

'Well, that's too bad, but I've got an unerring nose for shit.'

Maybe I've dreamed what happened next but I have a mental picture of Reed staggering back and throwing a protective arm across his face. It goes without saying that he was a thoroughgoing free thinker but he wasn't going to run any risk of being accidentally hit when the thunderbolts started whizzing around.

Sid's work got one of its earliest write-ups in *Angry Penguins* and it was quite a write-up. There's no signature but it can't have been produced by anyone except Reed. I recognise his tangled style. After some preliminary carolling, he bares his fangs and rips into people whose 'inner experience is so limited that they are completely incapable of extending their hidebound sensibility to embrace with enthusiasm the unknown message of the future which is revealed to them'. Why, that's me to the life, I exclaimed when I read it.

Reed was still groggy from my vile remarks about Sid's paintings when Dutton got uppity, too. Dutton was then a pilot in the RAAF, which inspired Sid to propose a rather scratchy drawing of an airfield. for the cover of his book. Without going as far as Reed in knee-bending adulation, Dutton was something of a fan of Sid's but as a pilot his professionalism was troubled by the fact that Sid had chosen to depict two airsocks blowing simultaneously in opposite directions. What Reed's reaction was when Dutton had the effrontery to mention this and suggest that the drawing be rectified I couldn't say. I imagine he was struck all of a heap. Someone present at the subsequent agitated conference, however, was able to report Sid's feelings. Dutton, he pronounced after brooding on the business a while, was 'an Air Force moron'. I, along with the rest of Dutton's friends, was delighted with the pithy description. We applied it to Dutton whenever we thought he was getting above himself.

I never learnt what kind of a moron Sid considered me. His face didn't exactly light up when he saw me but he was always chummy enough. He didn't seem to hold it against me that my hidebound sensibility was unable to embrace his secret message. Nor, as far as I could tell, did he share Reed's belief that anyone who failed to like his painting was headed for eternal damnation. He was credited with a County Wicklow temper but, even after I'd refused his jacket design, he never took his shillelagh to me.

As a matter of fact, he carried amiability to the point of wanting to make me a present of one of his paintings. None of us was in the habit of going easy on the others so I said flatly that I didn't want it. My tastes haven't changed but I wouldn't knock it back today. Whimpering among the unpaid bills and morosely totting up how much a painting by Sid now fetches, I've sometimes felt that it's a pity that we've lost touch and that it might be a friendly act to drop him a line. 'Dear Sid' (or would 'Dear Sir Sidney' be better?), 'On second thoughts I would like that painting of yours. Please forward, carriage paid, to the above address, and oblige ... '

Sid, I read a little while back in a rapturous newspaper article, is 'Australia's living national monument' so Reed has got his revenge. He maintained from the beginning that Sid was sublime and such is now the universal opinion. I didn't have the wit to know I was hobnobbing with a monument and can't even remember much about him.

In the end, Dutton and I got out own way. The windsocks were allowed to behave in accordance with the laws of anemology or whatever it is and Bert Tucker was allowed to design a jacket for my book which had me cavorting with an undiplomatic delight Reed found it hard to forgive. He punished me by refusing to let me have the original (for which I still bear him a grudge) and by stipulating that he would never speak to me again, so there. It was only the first of these penalties which caused me any real anguish.

To my surprise, I rate a mention m one of those 'Companions to Australian Literature' or 'Who's Who in Australian Letters' which apparently come out at the rate of one a week. Having made sure that I don't get too cocky by shaking his head over the 'lack of substance' in my poems, the writer of the entry in question goes on to say - with a touch of regret, unless I'm being too sensitive - that they were 'well received' when they first burst on the world. That isn't how I remember it. To the best of my recollection, neither I nor Dutton nor Roskolenko were received at all. The nearest any of us came to a rave review was a newspaper comment on the photograph of Dutton which served as a frontispiece to his book. It showed, so the journalist recorded, a cheerful looking young man in Air Force uniform (I think those were the very words) who would doubtless look back on his youthful verses with a tolerant smile when he was as old in years and wisdom as the journalist. The only other mention of us again featured Dutton.

It sounds like an *Angry Penguins* criticism. Dutton's poems, said whoever it may have been, were distinguished by their 'internal cohesion'. The tribute was read by one of Dutton's fellow pilots. 'You poor old bugger,' said this Air Force moron, 'I didn't know that you suffered from constipation.'

John and Sunday Reed at Heide, search for a figment in my imagination.

Top Sidney Nolan, Max Harris, Sunday and John Reed
in the Heide kitchen in 1945.
Above Sunday Reed with Joy Hester 1945.

CHAPTER FOUR

Ola Cohn, a Melbourne sculptress, was renowned for having carved the living daylights out of a tree in the Fitzroy Gardens. After she'd done with it, there were squirrels climbing the trunk, gnomes peeping out of holes, rabbits refuting the natural history textbooks by perching on the upper branches, elves, owls, pixies and every other manifestation of woodland whimsy which she'd been able to dream up. This object was known as the Fairy Tree and deserved it. But Ola was a kindly old girl and liked nothing better than to convene artistic gatherings at her East Melbourne studio.

It was at one of these that I made the acquaintance of Tom Lindsay, a hefty fellow with an engagingly satanic grin. He was one of the tentacular Lindsay clan, a distant relation of Norman's and Daryl's and Jack's although, unlike them, neither a painter nor a writer. He was no more than a lowly schoolmaster but that grin of his kept its promise and his ability to come out with entertainingly malevolent remarks appealed to me strongly. 'These confections of Ola's,' I remember him bellowing that evening so as to be audible to everyone present, including Ola, and at the same time gesturing towards our hostess's array of heads and torsos, 'all look like those fucking pixies of hers after being aborted on a brick pavement by an incompetent midwife.'

Anyone able to deliver a crack like that - and get away with it - was obviously to be cherished and I accepted with enthusiasm when, in the course of that first meeting, he invited me to have a drink a day or so later at the flat he occupied in St James's Buildings at the top end of Bourke Street. We had only just dipped into the first bottle and Tom had only just got off his first abominable remark of the day when a voice came pleadingly through the wall. 'Tom, can I borrow Lucy to suck Victor?'

I'd never heard a request so charged with interesting possibilities. I looked at Tom with a very wild surmise indeed. 'David', said Tom, as if that made everything clear. To my way of thinking, it didn't. Who was David, I asked, who was Victor, who was the compliant Lucy? And what frenzied bacchanal was about to get under way? David, Tom explained, grinning evilly, was David Strachan, the artist who had the studio next door, Victor was a carpet to which David was greatly attached, Lucy was Tom's vacuum cleaner. The intriguing words I had overheard were the standard formula whereby David asked to borrow the latter appliance. However, even if no orgy was due to take place, why didn't I help to transport Lucy to the waiting Victor and meet David myself?

By some quirk of memory, I have a Kodak image in my mind of the studio in which that initial meeting occurred. It was large and sunny with an immense floor- to-ceiling window. There were two easels and on a large table brushes were soaking in jam jars. Canvasses were leaning up against the walls. Exotic looking cloths were flung haphazardly on a couple of armchairs. Victor, as handsomely patterned as a python, sprawled across the floor. Books and clay figures and miscellaneous oddities were randomly jumbled together on the chimney piece. I'd read Murger and Du Maurier and Dorian Gray. If anyone knew down to the last detail what an authentic art-for-art's-sake-and-to-hell-with-the-bourgeoisie studio ought to look like, it was me. I had the sort of ingenuous romantic feeling about studios that one's entitled to have at eighteen and this was high romance if ever I'd come on it.

The studio, the genuine *Vie de Boheme* studio, gave me a tremendous kick (not that I let on, of course) but I was frankly intimidated by David. He was only two years older than I, which meant that he was no more than nineteen or twenty when Tom first introduced us. He was, however (or so I thought), alarmingly mature and worldly. It was clear that he found it altogether natural to be living in a studio (with a floor-to-ceiling window, what's more) and his urbane self-possession made a depressing contrast with my just-left-school *gaucherie*. Dressed in paint-splattered and well-worn clothes, there was nonetheless a certain dandyism about him. When I discovered that, young as he was, he had already studied at the Slade in London and had actually visited Paris (a smuggled copy of *Ulysses* attested to this), my sense of inferiority was complete. I went zooming in my own estimation down into the bargain basement.

If David shared this low opinion of me, he never let it appear. On the contrary, he behaved as if he genuinely liked me and since we continued to see a good deal of each other I presume he did. I was glad to think that he considered me a friend, because I took to him from the outset. He laughed readily, which was something I valued in people. He was one of those who made Melbourne fun to be in. I never knew him morose. He not only laughed himself but he had a great gift for provoking laughter. It's true that his humour tended to be corrosive but since I was never on the receiving end, that was no problem. Nobody could do a better job of scraping the skin off someone he disliked with a single feline sweep of his claws. I was made aware of this deft malice of his at our first meeting. Tom happened to mention a painter known for his pernickety and bloodless style. 'Renoir used to say he painted with his penis', David remarked in the peculiar wailing voice which he habitually employed when preparing to make one of his merciless jabs. 'So-and-so obviously paints with his one remaining pubic hair.' It still amuses me as a witticism and to anyone familiar with the painter so expertly flayed it is a wonderfully succinct and accurate criticism. These scabrous sallies weren't to everybody's taste. They were to mine.

But it wasn't solely or even mainly on account of his pleasing wit that I liked and respected David. What appealed to me most was his blithe indifference to cults, fashions and theories in the arts and in life. If he'd decided that he wanted to paint in the manner of Alma-Tadema, the resulting derision and denunciation wouldn't have troubled him in the least. Not even the disapproval of that stout anti-clerical Gino would have deterred him if he'd wanted to become a Roman Catholic or a Seventh Day Adventist. His communist acquaintances had made sporadic attempts to enlist him in the service of their ridiculous cause. They merely provoked his laughter. He and Adrian were alike in that they were unshakably attached to their freedom as artists and individuals. It explains much of the hostility they both aroused among the political and artistic automata.

Presumably, anyone with no eye for the beauty of Sid Nolan's achievements is automatically disqualified from having any opinion on art. John Reed, I'm confident, would have wanted to have it made illegal for any such scoundrel to say anything about anything ever again. So I'm undoubtedly harming David's reputation by admitting that I very much admired his work then and do now. Someone sneered that he and one or two others constituted the 'Charm School'. Very droll, I dare say, except that I've never understood why the possession of charm has come to be regarded as tantamount to suffering from bad breath. A number of Ezra Pound's early poems (and they're among the best he wrote) could be prosecuted on the same grounds, I take it, and so could some of Ravel's music. Myself, I'll go on reading those poems and listening to that music whatever the cultural vigilantes have to say about it.

Possibly the little jibe about charm meant simply that David and his friends could draw (and if Sid is the standard by which everyone's work is to be judged, that's already a black mark against them) and that they had a defective social conscience which showed itself in a reluctance to portray exhausted coal miners leaving the pithead or haggard slum children propped against leprous walls.

At irregular intervals David's studio was shared by his friend Wolf - Wolfgang Cardamatis, another member, according to the austere critic, of the charm school. Wolf, so I'm told, has become respectable, even devout. It's hard to believe. In his unregenerate youth, he was as respectable as Gilles de Retz. His face gave him away from the word go. And yet, now I come to think of it, there was always something that can only be described as beatific about the happy wickedness of his expression. 'Man, woman or dog, I throw it on a bed' was one of his recurrent declarations of faith. I don't know how the dogs made out; the rest of his claim chimes in pretty well with my recollections of him ...

He lived off and on with a young woman called Mabel who was intermittently the wife of the cartoonist Unk White, a star of the old *Smith's Weekly*. She and Wolf had an apartment, if that's the word for two dilapidated rooms, high under the roof of an ancient building somewhere off (I think) Flinders Street. It was rather out of the way but friends visiting them for the first time had no difficulty in finding it. They just had to follow the noise of crashing plates and breaking glass. The brawls between Wolf and Mabel were grandiose affairs and to the uninitiated scary. After you got used to them, you simply walked into their flat without bothering to knock (you could have pounded on the door with both fists and nothing would have been heard amid the bombardment going on inside), dodged a flying saucer or two, and settled down with a book until the contestants became aware of your presence.

Throughout these apocalyptic conflicts Wolf would preserve his radiant smile, obviously loving every minute of them. The climax would usually arrive with Wolf, still with the same glowing smile on his face, cavorting elf-like out of the room, his final insult consisting, with a tattoo of rolled r's, of a disdainful, 'My dearrr, you'rrre nothing but a grrreat Arrrmenian peasant.' He never explained what was so objectionable about Armenians or peasants. Possibly they were associated in his mind with some dark tale communicated to him by his Greek forebears. Mabel, more prosaically Australian, contented herself with muttering, 'Little shit', after which she would hunt around for an unbroken glass or cup in which to serve wine to the audience.

Melbourne would have been a much duller place without Wolf. He was a thoroughly reprehensible harlequin who contributed an element of mad gaiety to our lives for which I continue to be grateful. He never set out to *epater la bourgeoisie*. No effort was needed. Scandalising the upright and godly while simultaneously delighting those who were neither upright nor godly was something that came naturally to him.

For reasons which I didn't understand at the time and still don't, a group of us were once bidden by a nice, well-mannered young man of our acquaintance to attend a cocktail party being given by his mother. He had implored us beforehand - Wolf in particular - to behave ourselves in the presence of Mum and her guests. We put on ties and promised to be good.

To begin with, things couldn't have gone better. We were a credit to those who'd brought us up. Tom Lindsay didn't make a single outrageous remark, David comported himself with the graceful civility to be expected of an Old Boy of Geelong Grammar and Wolf, to our astonishment, was handing around trays of *hors d'oeuvre*. Only not for long. A muted shriek proclaimed that something had gone wrong. What was wrong was Wolf's penis. He had placed that organ on a tray which he held at the appropriate level, decorated with lettuce and sliced beetroot so that it was practically concealed and was proffering it to one be-hatted matron after another. The first to take it delicately between thumb and forefinger was responsible for the horror-stricken yelp we had heard.

It appears that the identical scene was enacted in a film a year or so back. I call heaven to witness that the notion had crept into Wolf's ribald mind long before it had occurred to an emancipated Hollywood.

Nobody could have been more dissimilar to the exuberant Wolf than Albert Tucker. Of all the men I ever came across, he was the most serious-minded. That he underwent the most profound, and often the most devastating, emotional experiences is sufficient!y demonstrated by his paintings and as a man he was utterly unlike the purse-mouthed Reed he didn't consider it demeaning to laugh and, when not preoccupied with some interior crisis, he was cheerful company. But he was an intellectual, if ever there was one. He was also a man of high intelligence. Until I met him, I hadn't believed the combination was possible. The professed intellectuals I'd previously encountered - and, except for the flies, they were Australia's most prevalent pest - had been a joyless lot and irredeemable simpletons into the bargain, who could be relied on to entangle themselves in any thicket of nonsense that lay in their path.

The bulk of these dismal loons in my day were communists and in all likelihood, with their innate genius for seeing nothing and learning nothing, still are. You could only tell them apart - if you could tell them apart - by the fact that the homicidal tantrums to which they were prone sprang from different causes. There was Mr Smith the bounty hunter (you haven't forgotten Mr Smith?) forever hunting fascist Snarks. There was the painter Noel Counihan who couldn't bear the thought of all the money Sunday Reed had inherited (communists and the Left in general are vastly more obsessed with money than any of the top-hatted bankers spangled with dollar signs who were a constant feature of the Party's broadsheets). There was a writer called George Farwell who (but I may be wrong about this his arguments weren't always easy to follow) was very down on the censoring of any books except those written by people he disliked. Collectively, the whole bunch were for ever gazing popeyed right through the gulags and the KGB, seeing nothing but merry workers dancing to the sound of balalaikas when not beamingly engaged in building the Dnieper Dam. Slow on the uptake, the intellectuals ...

Where Bert was concerned, I was lamentably slow on the uptake myself. Unfortunately for me, because it delayed an acquaintanceship which I came to value greatly, I got it into my head that Bert belonged to this *lumpenintelligentsia*, that there was a whiff of Marxist brimstone about him. So there was; but what I idiotically failed to appreciate was that Bert had no reinforced-concrete certitudes. He was an admirer of D. H. Lawrence but I should think Lawrence's 'blood truths' were abhorrent to him. His intellectual probity was absolute. He could never, as I did, have kicked Marxism in the teeth after thirty seconds' nauseated contemplation nor, as Counihan and his cell mates did, entered into a state of religious ecstasy on first catching a glimpse of the Virgin Rosa Luxemburg in the sky. Bert was driven by the need to scrutinise every idea, every constituent element of an idea, before resolving to adopt it, reject it, or disregard it.

Marxism, he finally decided, to the surprise of no-one who knew his cast of mind, was not for him. He said as much, unequivocally. That took some doing. The local communists were blankly unable to comprehend that his austere intelligence was proof against any amount of manipulation, intimidation or cajolery. He had investigated Marxism with the same rigour he would have applied to the analysis of any other problem. The communists, so easily bamboozled themselves, couldn't believe that Bert, having been brought face to face with the *ipsissima verba*, would refuse to capitulate.

As he'd most certainly anticipated, the posse went after him at a breakneck gallop. The people's justice! Vyshinsky wasn't in it. They could hardly hope to get away with an allegation that Bert, who'd never had a cent in his life, had inherited a fortune like Sunday Reed but the boys were never at a loss for long. Writing in one of the Party's ragbags, Noel Counihan put everyone right about the facts of the case. Bert, the 'political theroetician' (would that have been a misprint or a doughty display of contempt for bourgeois spelling?), along with Max and Sidney Nolan and Reed, had 'adopted a more and more anti-working class, anti-Soviet position'. Nobody could sink lower than that.

The indictment was more than Reed could bear. *Angry Penguins* published his defence. Hadn't he used his own and his wife's money to support the Communist Party election campaign? Hadn't he dipped into the same treasury in order to give a helping hand to one of the Party's top men? Hadn't he, as co-editor of *Angry Penguins*, published the work of Party members in good standing? He had indeed, the poor booby, and for the life of him he couldn't make out why the lads were so ungrateful. His simplicity was sometimes, truly disarming.

Bert was a tougher proposition. The Party didn't succeed in wringing any 'confessions' from him or any thin reedy cries for forgiveness. It's likely that he never rid himself of his 'social awareness' and I doubt if he would have wanted to. He had known poverty at first hand and he had an intense compassion in his make-up; but he had done with political theories (theroies?) for good. He had adopted, as Counihan would have said, a more and more individualistic position; and it's true that nothing could be more anti-Soviet than that.

I hadn't been in touch with Bert for thirty-odd years. I wrote to him the other day in an attempt to straighten out some of my contorted memories and in his reply he mentioned in passing that 'I have a copy of your revised version of *The Denunciad* which you sent me when you realised that I wasn't a commy ratbag after all - but I assume you have the original of that.' I don't. I don't have the unrevised version, either, but I can recall enough of it to feel remorseful.

The Denunciad was a pugnacious pasquinade which, according to Richard Haese in his book about Australian rebels, 'roused a great deal of laughter'. I didn't hear any, except from Adrian who'd given the thing its title. One or two of those I'd aimed at took it without rancour. Bert was one of these, but there was one couplet which, he subsequently told me, had fretted him .

> *. . . where Albert Tucker lives*
> *Deep in the cleft of split infinitives*

'Where', Bert asked me almost as soon as we were on speaking terms, 'did I split infinitives?'

'Nowhere as far as I know.'

'Then ... ?'

The truth of the matter was that the lines had occurred to me as faintly amusing and I'd tacked them on to the first name that came to mind. It would have been immeasurably more satisfying if I could have used John Reed for the purpose (he handled the English language as expertly as a bushman operating a computer) or Noel Counihan or Mr Smith. The hitch was that their names wouldn't scan. So it was Bert, an admirable writer with an irreproachable style, who took the rap. It was deplorable behaviour on my part. Bert himself, sternly opposed to misrepresentation in any circumstances, would have been incapable of it. He forgave me but couldn't forbear to utter a mild protest.

'I've spent hours going through old articles trying to locate the split infinitives thanks to you. My God! The time I've wasted!'

Not everyone was as magnanimous as Bert. *The Denunciad* may well have been juvenile and inept but for sheer lack of discrimination it can't be faulted. I wiped the edge of my hand across practically every windpipe within reach, including those of the *Angry Penguins* group with which I was supposed to be associated (which didn't prevent an appreciative and generous Max from publishing it right there, in *Angry Penguins*). Looking back, I've not the least idea what set me going on this rampage. I had no particular reason - no reason whatever in most cases - for mauling this one or that. Clem Christesen, for instance - I'd got nothing against Clem. We'd never met but there'd been a perfectly amiable exchange of letters between us. He had been sufficiently well-disposed, if I'm not misremembering, to publish some poems of mine in an early issue of *Meanjin*. I'd been in correspondence, too, with Rex Ingamells and we hadn't squabbled. Nobody ever took me for one of the gumnut babies but Rex was tolerant enough to print one or two of my poems in his *Jindyworobak*. Still, there it was both of them got a pasting in *The Denunciad*.

I imagine that my motive in writing this scurrilous broadside was simply that I was looking for trouble - except that imagination doesn't come into it I know damn well I was looking for trouble. It duly came my way. John Reed, I think, had already carried out his threat never to speak to me again so that the lines devoted to him (I wish I hadn't let him off with a single couplet) probably made no difference to our relations. But all communication ceased thereafter between me and Christesen, between me and Ingamells, between me and ...

The communists en bloc (but they were always *en bloc*) took my quips very much amiss. That was just as it should have been. Teasing the comrades was a favourite pastime of mine - their reactions were so wonderfully wholehearted. I'd scored a win not long before when I had inexplicably been invited to address the Melbourne University Literary Society and had inexplicably accepted. It promised to be a lacklustre occasion for all concerned and I thought it might brighten up the proceedings if I sported a little with the Party-goers who were bound to attend in strength. My anti-Soviet slander took the form of drawing on a pair of surgical gloves before reading some muscular verses from a copy of *The International Ironworker* or *The Odessa Moonbeam* or whatever the periodical may have been called.

This, I don't need to be told, was scarcely the wittiest performance on record but the audience, most of it, was appalled by such irreverence and that, after all, had been the whole idea. The incident confirmed my reputation as a fascist reptile but for the present I escaped without a scratch. The only rejoinder was an account of the business in the university weekly paper. My gloves, it reported, had proved to be too small and I'd been ignominiously compelled to abandon my indecent buffoonery. Nothing of the kind the gloves fitted like - well, a glove.

Some years after I'd settled in France a letter arrived from Adrian...

"I gave a lecture to our Victorian Artists Society the other evening, and was accosted afterwards by one Noel Counihan, the 'Social Realist' painter and propagandist, as you may remember - you once slapped him in a lampoon. He was accompanied by several of his communist buddies, all very truculent and all wanting a piece of me, God knows why. And before one could say 'Kershaw!' he was covering you (along o' me) with a special gobful of vituperation, a slither of which went this way, verbatim 'Yah, Kershaw the fascist!' A. L. 'Ah, the charming Alister! A fascist, is he? What a pity I didn't know about that. I'm a fascist myself.' N. C. 'You're telling us! We knew that, too.' A. L. 'I say, the things you fellows know.' N. C. 'Yah, you're just a big bluff, like Kershaw!' A. L. 'Well, somebody has to do the bluffing ... '"

It was soothing to hear that the dear old familiar yahing and bahing vocabulary hadn't changed. It brought Melbourne very close.

David Strachan, *Self-portrait*, Melbourne 1938.

CHAPTER FIVE

Over the years I've done my best to evoke Adrian in books and articles and broadcasts and, as anyone will confirm who ever came within earshot of me, I've talked about him to, as some of my friends have protested, excess. Whether or not I'll have another opportunity to recall in print the astonishing jumping jack that he was depends on the whims of God and the publishing trade. As to talking about him, I'll persist in that until it's made illegal to do so.

It's easy enough to account for this pertinacity of mine. How could anyone who knew him not want to write or talk about the most improbable sport, in the etymological sense, ever to emerge in Australia or, I'll affirm with my last breath, anywhere else? Only where does it lead? Nowhere, is the answer to that one. Whenever I've attempted myself to depict him, to reproduce his whirligig conversation, to summon up his life-enhancing spirit, I've been driven to realise that I might just as well have tried to mummify a will-o'-the-wisp.

In spite of which, here we go again ...

A lot of unamiable terms were applied to him by the sort of people whose good opinion no-one with a sense of smell would want anyway. For the rest, he was habitually described as 'mercurial'. It doesn't go nearly far enough. Mercury is sluggish by comparison. Mentally and, with his conjurer's tricks of appearing and disappearing at will, physically as well, he was perpetual motion.

Bert was one of those who immediately perceived his quality. As he told an interviewer,

"Adrian had enormous energy, a high voltage personality and a rapier kind of intellect, going in and out on every issue at full speed. An extraordinary looking man and an extraordinarily energetic man, involved both with painting and ideas ... Through the thirties he was to me one of the more dominant figures, and ... is still underestimated. Adrian's role is underplayed all the way through. He was a very important man.

Things have changed a little since Bert gave that interview ten years ago. It's now recognised that there was such a man as Adrian Lawlor. In line with the convention that nobody is any good until he's in the grave, a posthumous exhibition of Adrian's work was held, with the appropriate flapdoodle, at the Heidi Art Gallery which had once been the Reeds' home. It was a comical site to pick because Adrian would never have been admitted to the Heidi ashram so long as Reed had enough strength to get to the telephone and call the police, and Adrian could never have been dragged past the door except under heavy sedation. Then, Richard Haese made a reasonable fuss of him in his *Rebels and Precursors* and Gavin Fry has published a small book about him. Not much in the way of attention but a lot more than was ever paid to him in his life-time.

I suppose Adrian and I would have met sooner or later - it was difficult in Melbourne in that epoch not to meet everybody whether you wanted to or not - but in the event it was Gino who brought us into contact. Gino had done me many good turns but never a better one than when he insisted that I should read Adrian's *Arquebus*. That was a day! Was it possible that such a wayward comic masterpiece had been produced in Melbourne, just around the corner? It was possible. I started to read it as I walked away from Gino's shop; I was laughing aloud before I'd gone ten yards. I've gone on laughing ever since and made plenty of other people laugh with me.

But I was for a long while in the quaint position of having to implore Adrian himself to relish *Arquebus* as much as I did. He hadn't looked at the book in years, had forgotten all about it, didn't particularly want to be reminded of a work which had been received with such formidable apathy - a roaring failure, he would probably have called it. I triumphed in the end, though, and he acknowledged as much in one of his incomparable letters

"I found myself the other day glancing through your letters - of which naturally I have retained every single one throughout these otherwise uneventful years - and I found to my amazement and embarrassment indeed that they contained (I had almost said invariably) references of a consistently eulogistic tone to my *Arquebus* (which, you may perhaps not remember, you were actually carrying in your hand on the occasion of our very first meeting!). What is it, I found myself driven to ask myself, what excuse is there for this constant, this continuously maintained, obsession on his part concerning this *jeu d'esprit* of mine farted (if you'll allow me to put it so) into the stuttering faces of that bygone horde of - Jesus! a generation ago. (If only I could express myself here in French good enough for your fastidious taste!) We all know - that is to say, he and I, the only readers the book has ever had - that it is good, of course; but what of that it's not as if Alister didn't know about books - he's read everything.

"And I crawled out of my rocking-chair and went across the room - to be precise, into the adjoining receptacle where the bookcase of paperbacks resides - to extract the only copy of the thing I have in my shelves, so that I could possess myself of it and see if you could possibly be anywhere near right in your estimate.

"Alister, I've read it three times with simple astonishment, even if prompted by your admiration of its character. I have given it all my thought (all our thought) for a whole week. I'll probably read it again for the sheer fun of it for I find like you apparently that repeated readings merely increase one's enjoyment of it.

"Do you know, I'd rather have written this box of tricks than any other book concocted in Australia; and I convey with that the admission that I am blissfully unaware of any of those books or who has written them.

"This'll do me! ..."

He was, as Bert says, an extraordinary looking man, with his cavernous cheeks, his improbably high forehead, his (because no other word will serve) mesmeric eyes, and an expression which changed as constantly, as rapidly, as iridescently as the sheen on a patch of oil, moving unpredictably from an immense melancholy to a bewildering gaiety. George Bell painted a portrait of him, so did Lina Bryans and William Frater and so, most successfully of all, did Bert himself. But nobody, in whatever medium, had a hope of snaffling or lassoing so intransigent a creature.

His 'Collected Letters' - but collected, tumbled together, without regard to chronological or any other order and left unblotched with explanatory footnotes - would provide the only portrait worth having, a living self-portrait. I must have had hundreds of letters from him in the course of our long friendship, every one of them what Shapiro would have called a shot in the arm, read and re-read and read again. If the whole collection hadn't been pinched long since, I could have saved myself a lot of work and given the reader the impression that he was really getting something for his money simply by filling the rest of this book with them.

It would have been still better if I could have recorded all of those flying trapeze discourses which swung him and his listeners in wild eccentric parabolas. He was, in his talk, funambulist, acrobat and juggler at one and the same time. A record, a single record, did once exist, replete with the gags, puns, allusions and euphuisms, the leaps and bounds which made up his every utterance. I had just finished making a recording for the ABC on one of the friable 'acetate' discs which were used before tape-recorders hit the market when Adrian unexpectedly walked into the studio.

'Gahd! The *gadgets* here! What do you do with them? Or, which is more likely (life being what it is and none of us secured from external disaster) what do they do with you? Is the very chair on which you sit an electric chair? Those switches, those buttons! There used to be a children's ditty, a catch, a round - American, would it have been? - the querulous burden of which was "Button, button, who's got the button?" And now we know. You have.'

'Not my buttons, Adrian. They're the sole responsibility of the engineer.'

'The engineer hoist with his own button, I conjecture.'

'He's a sound engineer.'

'Any why, will you tell me, should he not be sound, sound to the core? Are engineers to be dismissed, on account of their profession merely, as *unsound*, flawed, faulty in their principles and lax in their morals? What aberration is this?'

'Adrian, while you're here - what about you making a record?'

'I? I'll have no part of any such lackwit scheme. Nay, from the tables of my memory I'll wipe away all trivial fond records. Well, perhaps not all. I'd miss the Last Quartets - nothing trivial about them.'

'Come on. I'll bear you company. We'll do a cross-talk act.'

'Not for Cadwallader and all his goats. I'd rather discuss, unrecorded, these buttons of yours. *Revenons a nos boutons.*'

A protracted wrangle followed. Finally, I managed to persuade him. There was uproarious stuff on that record, interspersed with protracted spasms of laughter from Adrian, overcome with the preposterous, the totally impossible, notion that every word he said was actually being recorded and could be heard again by himself whenever the whim took him. It was his first and last incursion into a world where such things happened.

I interrupted one of his paroxysms.

'Go on talking, Adrian, blast you. We're wasting time. That damned disc is spinning round at a rate of seventy-eight revolutions per minute.'

And from Adrian, writhing in an attempt to repress his incredulous merriment, 'Is it? Is it by God? I wondered why I felt so *giddy*!'

The record, the unique record, was purloined along with the letters so that nobody, except for a handful of privileged dotards like myself, will ever know what it was to be hurtled around - at incalculably more than seventy-eight revolutions per minute - by Adrian's headlong talk. It was bewitching - literally so because it exercised, and on the most unlikely people, an irresistible spell. How many times in how many pubs have I watched, in nail-biting apprehension, as Adrian, against all the odds, wove his magic around a group of stevedores, wharfies and truck-drivers. He would be telling the rest of us about, let's say, Proust. The adjacent drinkers would be listening without enthusiasm. Why the hell should they have to put up with this bullshit? Finally, their exasperation would overcome them. From one of them would come a threatening comment, as it might be 'Cop the bloody pansy!' and Adrian would turn unhesitatingly towards him. 'A Proustian, are you, my dear fellow? But on what do you base this assertion of yours? That Marcel might be described as a shrinking violet, I grant you, albeit he was never known to shrink from a coronet; but a pansy? Something of a less blatant colouring wouldn't you say?'

We'd watch the performance unbelievingly, however often we'd already seen it enacted in different forms. Within minutes Adrian would have his audience meekly soliciting further information about Proust.

'Well, you in particular, Len, will appreciate the primacy of the question that arises. It's evident that you are familiar with time, may, for all I could assert to the contrary, have *done* time. You have a supplementary qualification, however. Truck-driver that you are, you are acquainted with overtime. And here we must confront the dilemma. That Proust should write about mere time is well enough; that he should, as he did, overwrite about overtime is, you'll concur, a vastly different dish of tea or plate of madeleines.' Thereafter, one heard nothing from the truck-drivers and stevedores but a recurring and deferential 'Have another beer, Adrian.'

Well, the talk is gone for ever. What remains, apart from the paintings, are his two books. No-one who's read this far is going to be in any doubt as to what I think of *Arquebus* a magnificent rollicking satire which, if things were as they ought to be, would have been put back in print ages ago. What about his novel, Horned Capon? That would never have got into print at all if it hadn't been for Adrian's friend and mine, Denison Deasey. Deasey had money - a circumstance which endlessly fascinated Adrian for whom there was no significant difference between fifty cents and a million dollars. 'Tell us, Dease, how much have you got? A cool thou'? A pony?' Whatever it may have been, Deasey admired *Horned Capon* sufficiently to subsidise its publication.

That wasn't so easy. The war was over but the bloody-minded functionaries who'd had such enjoyment from imposing their rationing on a submissive public weren't going to relax their grip until they had to. Poor old Deasey tottered closer and closer to lunacy (and he was fairly lunatic to begin with) as he scrounged paper (and vile paper it was) from the ill-disposed 'authorities' and strove to convince his printer that the whole purpose of printers was to *print*. He and Adrian were unaffectedly astounded when the printer, much older and much richer by this time - and Deasey, of course, much older and much poorer - actually delivered the goods. From France I wrote to tell Adrian of my delight. He was pleased by what I had to say

'For this letter of yours contains, really you know, your first overt committal of opinion - of critical approbation - of a book (a BOOK, as you magnanimously cipher it!) which is now at last given flattering and multiplied appearance as a stack of volumes, whose too solid weight I found myself agonisingly wishing, yesterday, as I staggered fifteen several times up the six flights to my attic (myself my own self-begotten sorcerer's apprentice, as it were) would thaw and resolve itself into a bucket of hops. That I would gladly have undertaken to carry without spilling a drop - this side of the upstairs lavatory at any rate ...'

Horned Capon (there was nothing of the capon about it) was, as everyone except Adrian knew in advance it would be, given a thorough going-over by the rare reviewers who took any notice of it. A. D. Hope, in particular, berated it with hand-rubbing enjoyment. If he hadn't decided ever since his gunning down of Max that it was his life's mission to put writers in their place, he might have been able to see the book's merits. It has plenty. It's not as totally successful as *Arquebus,* I suppose, because Adrian's was essentially a comic genius, and comedy occurs only spasmodically in *Horned Capon*; and let's make Mr Hope happy by conceding that there are passages of bathos here and there. Nevertheless ...

There's a paragraph in a review by D. H. Lawrence of Corvo's *Hadrian the Seventh* which strikes me as peculiarly applicable to Adrian's equally erratic work

A man must keep his earnestness nimble, to escape ridicule. The so-called Baron Corvo by no means escapes. He reaches heights, or depths, of sublime ridiculousness. It doesn't kill the book, however. Neither ridicule nor dead earnest kills it. It is extraordinarily alive, even though it has been buried for twenty years. Up it rises to confront us. And, great test, it does not 'date' as do Huysmans' books, or Wilde's or the rest of them. Only a first-rate book escapes its date.

Sooner or later (later, presumably) some percipient publisher, I'm ready to bet, will bring out a new edition of *Horned Capon*. And why not, while he's at it, a new edition of *Arquebus*? Perhaps, in an ultimate spasm of acumen, he'll bring together the gyrating bits and pieces which are scattered through different reviews or which exist only in manuscript. I included one of the latter in a memoir of Adrian which the American printer R. T. Risk produced at his Typographeum Press. That an American should have been willing to publish a memoir of one unconsidered Australian writer by another rates, I'd say, a grateful tugging of forelocks and dipping of lids. But it's a pity that nobody in Australia gave any indication of wanting to take it on.

Adrian's appearance was, to repeat Bert's adjective again, extraordinary; his disappearances were twice as extraordinary and infinitely more disconcerting. Nobody could have been more blazingly present than Adrian when the atmosphere was sympathetic. He was always the star turn wherever he happened to be. His abhorrence of 'parties' - we were great throwers of parties then - was unabounded, but every so often he could be wheedled into turning up at some do or other. It would be all wrong to say that he took the floor. He didn't have to take it. It was enough for him to start talking and within minutes the entire company would be grouped in an awe-struck circle around him. 'How Adrian's enjoying himself', we'd tell each other. Was he? No.

Sometimes we'd be given warning that he was about to dematerialise by a barely audible mutter of 'What am I *doing* here?' More often, no warning whatsoever was given. Either way, abruptly there'd be no more Adrian, not a sign of him. He wasn't seen to detach himself from his admirers, to cross the floor, to go through the door. He simply wasn't there any more. Without any Wellsian mumbo jumbo he possessed the art of making himself invisible.

In that memoir of mine I recalled one such spooky occasion. It can illustrate the scores of others I saw - or, if you prefer, didn't see. We were on a bus going to Adrian's house in Warrandyte. The passengers were mostly businessmen commuting homewards at the end of a day's stockbroking or whatever their occupation may have been. Adrian gave his opinion of them. It was unfavourable. He stared around with a mixture of resentment and misgiving. I recognised the symptoms. My diagnosis was right. The conductor was making a tour of the bus collecting fares. He collected from the man next to me, he collected mine, he walked straight past Adrian. All he'd seen was an empty seat. Adrian had vanished.

Eva, Adrian's gentle and adoring wife, died. A second marriage ended catastrophically. When Deasey went to see him at Warrandyte, he was greeted, so he told me, with the words, 'Why have you come here? I'm dead.' This became, I also heard, his unvarying reply to anyone who, on his rare visits to Melbourne, tried to speak to him 'Don't talk to me. I'm dead.'

Then, in order to give some financial help to his sister, he sold the house at Warrandyte and shifted to a small flat in the suburbs, seeing nobody, no longer painting, no longer writing. And then he disappeared for the last time.

SIX

Max Nicholson is written up in Richard Haese's book as someone playing a 'self-appointed role of guide and mentor' among us. That was news to me. I never saw him guiding. On the other hand, when Haese goes on to describe him as 'a lively presence on the Melbourne art and intellectual scene', you won't find me kicking. Lively is what he was all right.

When I knew him he lived in a Carlton loft which, on request, he would place at the disposal of friends who had come to a satisfactory arrangement with a young woman but who had nowhere in which to do anything about it. At the foot of the rickety stairs Max would signal that he would like to resume occupancy by thumping vigorously with the walking stick which he invariably carried in those days. A dismissive grunt from the temporary occupant would result in his stalking obligingly away, only returning when he felt that enough time had elapsed for any reasonable libido to be satisfied. There must be a number of survivors apart from myself who remember the loft with tender affection and Max with gratitude.

This serviceable place of Max's was situated not far from Melbourne University, an institution from which since graduating he had some difficulty in detaching himself. He was usually in attendance at whatever meetings of the various clubs and societies were being held and he was also a conspicuous figure by reason of his involvement with the 'Back to the Horse Movement' of which he was founder, honorary president, secretary and sole member. When the mood took him, he would bestride with considerable panache an antique nag which was tethered near the University gates and which was ordinarily used to drag a roller over the cricket pitch. Mounted on this forlorn creature he would proceed to amble a few yards while groups of bemused students looked on. 'The horse, dear boy,' Max would proclaim magisterially, 'it's our abandonment of the horse that lies behind the anguish of the modern psyche.'

He was much given to apophthegms of this nature which he would apply to the most incongruous circumstances and which somehow became increasingly droll the more he repeated them. 'It's all in Freud' was one such dictum.

'I've got a terrible toothache.'

'Of course you have, dear boy. It's all in Freud.'

'And my dentist has just gone on holiday, damn him.'

'Naturally, naturally, it's all in Freud.'

At one point Freud was ousted by Kafka although no reason was ever given by Max for this change of allegiance. He made perilous use of the new maxim one evening when half a dozen of us had gone to the cinema. In the middle of the main feature, Max uttered a strident cry of alarm. He'd dropped a priceless diamond on the floor, he explained. No diamond existed outside Max's fancy, inflamed as it was by the plonk we'd all been drinking earlier, but there was no convincing Max of this. On all fours, he began hunting for his mythical diamond down one row of seats and up another. You could see people rising agitatedly as he crawled over their feet and you could hear Max repeating soothingly, 'Nothing to worry about, my dear sir, looking for a diamond - it's all in Kafka, all in Kafka.'

Max never informed us whether he considered Deasey to be all in Freud or all in Kafka. Probably both. Deasey (he was Deasey even to his intimates; no-one ever used his Christian name) was a sad, delightful, intolerable man. His sadness, I think, derived largely from the fact that he had an intense feeling for all the arts and was essentially unequipped to practise any of them. Every effort he made to do so was that of an amateur.

He was delightful, among other reasons, because, a frustrated artist himself and resentful of his incapacity, he was generous in encouraging the people he admired. He bought paintings from artists who hadn't at that time many purchasers queueing up to buy their work Arthur Boyd was one of them. Adrian's *Horned Capon*, as I've already mentioned, would never have been published without Deasey's enthusiasm and money. When, in 1947, along with the rest of the gang, I wanted to go to Europe, Deasey volunteered to pay my fare (I haven't often danced a jig when repaying a debt but the time came when Deasey was no longer the nabob he had been and that debt I settled without a sob).

The intolerable side of him was mainly due to a smouldering temper which was likely to burst into flames at any moment and for no discoverable cause. Sid Nolan had nothing on him. 'Whenever Deasey's around', our friend Dorian Le Gallienne used to say plaintively, 'I feel like one of those innocent bystanders you read about in newspapers.' In all fairness, you couldn't blame Dorian for being uneasy. Deasey's Hibernian outbreaks were impressively comprehensive. He'd start by bestowing a few incivilities on an unknown and, as far as anyone else could see, harmless drinker in a pub. One of us, hoping to prevent a major donnybrook, would say something placatory. Forthwith, Deasey would drop his original victim and turn gloweringly on the peacemaker. By the time he'd finished, everyone in the place would have been the object of his vituperation. A difficult fellow, in short You never knew when, where, why or on whom his ire would descend next. One thing, however, you could be sure of - at any given moment Deasey would not be on speaking terms with two-thirds of his friends.

I was one of the two-thirds at frequent intervals, but for me Deasey's appealing qualities outnumbered those of his characteristics which periodically made one yearn to garrotte him. A bond was established between us very early on when we were driving in his open Bentley. For some reason we were going practically at walking pace - a pace foreign to Deasey who normally conducted his juggernaut at a speed in the region of eighty mph. All of a sudden, a tarantula emerged from God knows where and proceeded to crawl across the windscreen. With no word exchanged between us and without pausing to open the doors, Deasey vaulted out his side and I vaulted simultaneously out mine. The Bentley rolled, with only the tarantula in charge, until it came to rest against a tree. I could never thereafter, infuriating as he was, feel a lasting annoyance with a man who was as craven as I was in the matter of tarantulas.

We also shared a sense of humour, if that's what it was, which manifested itself in a variety of idiotic 'acts'. The bulk of our friends regarded these as embarrassingly schoolboyish but we thought they were incomparably funny. My own clowning mostly revolved around a gigantic but imaginary dog called Grendel. For some reason, Grendel showed a great reluctance to enter pubs so I would stand just inside the door, huffing and puffing - in an effort to drag the animal across the threshold while the company waited to see what colossal object was going to appear. Eventually, I'd overcome Grendel's obstinacy, bend down to give him an appreciate pat on his invisible head, order him to sit (occasionally I'd have to give him a sharp cuff or even a kick before he'd obey) and ask the barman for a dish of water 'for my pet'. Depending on the degree of alcoholism they'd attained, the customers would conclude that I was a (possibly dangerous) maniac or that they themselves had d.t.s.

Looked at dispassionately, there's no getting away from the fact that Deasey's favourite act was superior to mine in every way. In buses, in trains, in cafes and pubs, wherever there was a suitable public, he would adopt a leer of indescribable malignancy (his features were phenomenally elastic) and, in a macabre high-pitched whine which he had invented for the purpose, would narrate the doings of the day.

'A lovely day I've had,' he'd say so as to be clearly heard by everyone in the vicinity, 'a truly rewarding day. I was dissecting some kittens - oh, they were so pretty - no anaesthetic, of course - I always say you can't get the same effect if you use an anaesthetic. Then in the afternoon, I went to see my nephew. Dear little romper and, just think, with eight fingers on either hand. I always call him "Spider Boy". It's a family trait, too, and, oddly enough, no ears. I'd like to round the day off really nicely. What about coming with me to the morgue?'

Staider characters than ourselves weren't above indulging in similar antics. Dutton in Air Force uniform and Deasey in his army khakis were sometimes to be seen masquerading as military police. Their prisoner was invariably Arthur Boyd, who would put on a virtuoso performance, howling and struggling helplessly with his two towering captors. Onlookers were appalled by the extreme and unnecessary brutality shown to the unhappy Arthur. His screams were heart-rending.

Deasey's endowments included a noteworthy skill in the composition of occasional verses. He was not the only one. Dutton and I jointly produced some admirably indelicate lines on the Reeds and their friends of which the world must be deprived so long as the libel laws remain in force. On my own account, I wrote a valedictory poem when Dutton was posted to New Guinea and I'm inclined to give myself the pleasure of quoting the opening quatrain, which is all I can remember of it. 'Gat', it should be noted, was Dutton's affectionate term for the .22 rifle with which he made a nuisance of himself to any parrots ('pollies') he encountered while strolling over the family estate.

> Intrepid Dutton! Lift thy gat anew,
> Aim with the surest aim since time began.
> In Freedom's cause employ thy twenty-two
> Against the crafty pollies of Japan

I seem, by copying out this morsel, to have given myself a mnemonic jolt and recovered the last quatrain, too, although I would have sworn it had been erased from my memory forever. The reference in the final line is to that portentous review of Dutton's book of poems which I quoted earlier.

> Birdman and poet, let my numbers sound
> A clarion call to sing thee to the war
> And in thy common task and daily round
> May'st thou cohere internally yet more.

Feeble rubbish, no doubt, but if nothing else, it may serve to set off to advantage Deasey's bush ballad, *The Lament of an Afghan Hawker*, which included a truly inspired flight.

> Oh, take me back to Ispahan,
> Its mosques and its bazaars
> And to hell with all the Kellys
> And the everlasting stars.

It was neither Dutton nor I, however, for all our pretensions as poets, nor the gifted amateur Deasey, who flipped up to the top of Parnassus. That was the achievement of our friend Robert Southey (although I've sometimes surrendered to the temptation to claim the authorship myself)

    The notorious Senator Brewster
    Attempted to bugger a rooster
      An account of their fuck
      As described by Pearl Buck
    Will be published by Simon and Schuster.

Robert's illustrious forebear and namesake, we all agreed, had never done anything as good.

His friends were surprised, some of them incredulous, when Deasey announced that he was getting married. He seemed ill-suited to domesticity. The girl he'd fallen for belonged to what passed in Melbourne as high society - the kind of people who ate *foie gras* as casually as the rest of us ate meat pies. Deasey and I had only read about *foie gras*. One evening when his family-in-law were out of the way and we were investigating the pantry we came on ten or twelve large tins of the stuff - genuine *Foie gras aux truffes*. It was a big moment. We got to work with the opener. The *foie gras* itself looked okay but there was a sinister inky substance on the surface.

'Shit, it's gone bad! Open another.'

The next one had the same black blob on it, so had the next and the one after that. We opened them all. They'd all gone bad. We threw the whole lot, cursing, in the garbage can. Somebody should have told us that truffles were *meant* to look like that.

His family-in-law never really cared much for Deasey after this incident. To tell the truth, they hadn't much cared for him before. His own family were thoroughly acceptable and, without being in the *foie gras* class, Deasey himself had a substantial private income. But nobody in a radius of fifty miles was unaware of his knock-'em-down temper, his drinking habits were celebrated, and, above, all, he kept the most unfortunate company.

It wouldn't have been so bad if he'd huddled his friends out of sight. He didn't. He actually invited them to his very, very posh wedding. On one side of the church were the bride's guests, morning-suited or primly robed; on the other were Deasey's buddies, largely comprising a tatterdemalion troupe of writers and painters and whatnot. Adrian helped things along by commenting audibly on the organ music.

'Listen-Bach! Lovely! That's Deasey's doing, I warrant you. *Dah-di, dah-di, dah-dah-di, dah-do-di-do-dah.* You wouldn't get Bach from the charming nonentities over there. Not that I'm criticising you, my dear sir, nor you, madam. I'm merely rejoicing in our own friend Deasey's Bach - much to be preferred, you'll agree, to his bite.'

All that remained was for Deasey himself to do something unruly; and of course he obliged. A female gossip columnist was present. The previous week she had written a malicious item about him. He raised the issue with her in the garden where the wedding breakfast was being held. The conversation became heated. She was standing with her back to an ornamental pool ...

I accompanied Deasey on his honeymoon. A great plangent wail of outrage rose at once from Melbourne's better homes. There was a thin note of guilty delight to be heard as well. It wasn't every day that a scandal like this one was served up. Among our own acquaintances there was equally no doubt that an orgy of Babylonian dimensions was taking place. Opinions varied, however, as to the exact nature of the frolic. Did it involve Deasey and me, me and Deasey's wife qr the three of us in what might appropriately be called an all-embracing carnal tangle?

Deasey's wife was an exceptionally attractive young woman and I couldn't have asked for anything more delicious than the second of these arrangements. Unfortunately, the idea had occurred to no-one except, in brief salacious reveries, me. This misbegotten jaunt of ours was the product of innocence rather than unavowable lusts. We simply hadn't considered the possibility that anyone might find it suspicious.

A day or so after the wedding the phone had rung. 'That you, Ali? What about coming round for a drink?'

'Where the hell are you? I thought you were off in the country on your honeymoon.'

'Yeah, well we've been lumbering around the country for three days and it's a bloody bore. It'd be all right if we could do what you're supposed to on a honeymoon for twenty-four hours a day but who can? So we're back in town. I need someone to talk to. Hold on a minute. J. wants a word with you.'

J. came on the line.

'Do come round, Ali. Deasey's in a filthy mood.'

Over the drink Deasey had his bright idea.

'Look, J.'s old mum is screeching that we've got to bugger off again. According to her, you can't have a honey-moon in the city - it's got to be somewhere in the bush, for Christ's sake. I can't face a week of just J. and me in the bush. We'd both go crazy. Why don't you come with us?'

'Jesus, I can't do that, Deasey.'

J. seconded the proposal.

'Ali, you've got to come with us. Deasey's right. If we're on our own we'll kill each other.'

So off the three of us went, with not a wicked thought between us.

It was a pleasant week we spent. With someone to talk to, Deasey was in a buoyant mood. We had some good meals and drank some good wine and laughed plentifully. At night, J. and Deasey retired to their room in this or that inn and I retired to mine. There was no toing-and-froing during the night. *Honi soit* ...

Being married to Deasey must have been as reposeful as wrestling with alligators. J. stood it for longer than could have been expected from any normal human being. Fearful of provoking one of Deasey's harmless but awe-inspiring rages, she mostly preserved a prudent silence. She was an intelligent girl but she rarely ventured to voice an opinion. Once, however, she did speak up and the effect on Deasey was, as they say, salutary, although not for long.

He and I were discussing Eliot's *Sweeney Among the Nightingales*. We analysed the heli out of it. But both of us (and I've never been able to account for this weird blind spot) admitted to finding the very first word puzzling. 'Apeneck Sweeney ... ' What precisely had the Master intended to convey?

Deasey was of the opinion that the stress was to be laid on the second syllable - apeneck. 'It's clearly a Joycean word play. "Pen" symbolising the artist and at the same time implying that he is rewarded parsimoniously - with a penny, in fact.'

I wasn't able to concur.

'No, Deasey. The stress is on the first syllable-Apeneck. I agree about the word play but the reader instinctively thinks not of "pen" but of the Appenines."

We debated the question for some considerable time, J. listening, we hoped appreciatively.

'I suppose I'm being stupid as usual,' she said when there was a pause in the two thinkers' discussion. 'I would have thought it was just apeneck - you know, the neck of an ape.'

That was the only interpretation that had never occurred to us. For a moment, Deasey was consternated. Then he rallied bravely. 'Don't be so bloody silly, J. You don't know what you're talking about.'

When J. left the room a little while afterwards, he looked at me with an expression of profound anxiety. 'Jesus, if anyone ever tells her she was right my bloody authority is gone for good.'

Top: Alister with Geoffrey Dutton (centre) and Denison Deasey (right)
Above: Netta Aldington, Alister with Max Nicholson (right).

SEVEN

You've got every right to ask who was (or were) this 'we' that's been cropping up on every page. It suggests a horrible homogeneity and chumminess as if all the writers, painters and composers in Australia cohered in a gelatinous mass like the Pre-Raphaelite Brotherhood. You wouldn't have thought so if you'd heard Dutton giving tongue on the subject of John Reed or John Reed on the subject of Adrian. Take it from me, there was nothing fraternal about Adrian's estimate of Sidney Nolan, or Max Harris's of P. R. Stephensen, or practically anyone's of me.

Sir Robert Menzies' proposal to set up his no-nonsense Royal Academy gave rise to a Night of the Long Knives which had the good guys slicing up the bad guys and vice versa. When the social realists tried, in the name of Soviet-Australian friendship and the greater glory of Stalin, to take over the Contemporary Arts Society, and John Reed mounted the barricades to stop them, you could hear the resultant caterwauling from the Leonardo Book Shop to the Petrushka Cafe.

What I'm getting at is that maybe the gang warfare wasn't as ferocious as it was, and still is, among the ateliers of Paris - no-one, for instance, was actually murdered in Australia over divergent views concerning so-and-so's impasto or what's-his-name's chiaroscuro - but there wasn't an atmosphere of unalloyed loving kindness either. The lucky ones were those who could participate in what Haese calls the 'art scene' without becoming potential targets. Deasey was one of these. Erik was another.

One day I answered the telephone to hear a thick foreign voice asking deferentially whether I was the disting-

distinguished poet. That was an old gag. We were in the habit of working off such pleasantries on each other. Who was it this time? Deasey? Dutton? Max?

'Yes, this is the distinguished poet all right - and a bloody sight more distinguished than you'll ever be.'

'Of course, thank you very much. It is indeed because of your distinction that I take the liberty to incommode you in this informal manner. My esteem for your work is of the highest.'

'So it ought to be.'

'I have been wondering if I would not exceed permissible limits by inviting you to take lunch with me?'

'Listen, you stupid bastard whoever you are, I'll meet you at the Mitre at half past twelve. And you can do the paying.'

At the place and hour, a young sandy-haired Dutch soldier approached me hesitantly.

Soldier? Australian troops weren't celebrated for their spit-and-polish appearance but this was something such as I'd never seen before. His forage cap was on back to front, metal insignia hung by a single insecure thread from his shoulders, the cuff of one trouser leg was caught up in his wrinkled sock, both bootlaces were undone, his shirt buttons were all in the wrong buttonholes. He had not shaved for at least forty-eight hours.

'Mr Kershaw?'

'Was that you who rang up?'

'Exactly so. My name is Schwimmer.' It wasn't, as a matter of fact, but since, like so many others, he's sunk into a condition of dismal respectability, the square thing is to give him an alias and Schwimmer is near enough to his real name.

Private Erik Schwimmer of the Netherlands Army. None of us ever became accustomed to the notion of Erik as a soldier. Neither did Erik. Whoever dragooned him into the forces must have cursed the day. *All* his superiors, from corporal to general, must have cursed the day. Not that he was deliberately insubordinate or determined to destroy the morale of the Dutch army. He was simply incapable, psychologically, of conforming to any rules except those he'd set for himself.

At one point - or so the story went - the higher-ups cracked. They resolved to turn Erik into something resembling a soldier even if it meant that the rest of the war effort had to come to a stop. A sergeant, two corporals and a lance corporal were entrusted with the impossible mission.

Marching, it was decided, should be the first priority.

'Left,' bawled the sergeant, '*left*, right, *left*, right *left*, right, *left*, right.' Erik caught on to the significance of the stressed 'left' immediately. Anxious to please, he slammed his left foot to the ground with the relentless force of a road-rammer and a moment later lowered his right foot with the unnatural delicacy of a ballerina tiptoeing in *Swan Lake*. The sergeant, clenching his fists to stop himself from screaming, tried in vain to convince Erik that this wasn't what he had in mind. Erik persisted with his lopsided gait to the end, totally unable to see what he was doing wrong.

'There was an incontestable lack of logic in their orders,' he explained to us later (he was always very strong on logic). 'Had they placed an equal emphasis on the words, I would naturally have followed the same stresses with my feet. If they did not want an emphatic "left" and a markedly less emphatic "right" they should not have given their instructions in the form they did.'

He was dead serious. No militarist myself, I nonetheless felt a pang of compassion for the sergeant. According to the rumour that went around, after giving up on Erik he volunteered for a suicide operation. Nobody ever knew what happened to the corporals. Erik went on walking

Erik Schwimmer in 1944.

the way he'd always walked and dressing as he'd always dressed.

I don't remember how Erik came to be in Australia. Perhaps he never told me. Perhaps he didn't know himself. What mattered was that he did get there. His presence was a permanent source of pleasure to us. He had a genuine love of literature and had read widely in English, especially English poetry. But he was still making discoveries which he was eager to pass on. He would burst in dancing with excitement to tell us about something which had lost all its magic for us because we'd known it since childhood but which came to Erik fresh-minted.

'"If music be the food of love, play on!" Wonderful, wonderful! How could you have missed it?'

'But I didn't miss it, Erik. I've known it all my life.'

'Then why did you not tell me about it?'

His enthusiasm was immensely invigorating and he gave a fillip to our vanity (which, God knows, didn't need any fillip) by showing as much interest in what we were writing as in what Shakespeare had written. That was enough in itself to make him welcome.

'The other evening,' Erik told me one day, 'I was walking down Collins Street and a strange man was coming the other way so I stepped aside to make way for him. But he stepped aside too, so we were still face to face. So I stepped aside again and he did the same. Once again we were face to face.'

What was coming next, I wondered. It could scarcely have been a pick-up. An endearing loon, Erik, but I couldn't imagine that he was likely to appeal even to the most lecherous of the local homos.

'So I said, "I beg your pardon, sir. If you will stand still for a moment I will step aside or, if you prefer, I will stand still while you step aside"' (Erik's passion for logic again) "and we will be enabled to go on our ways." Then he said, "I know who you are. You are Private Schwimmer. But you can no longer be private because I wish to talk to you." And I said, "May I know who you are, sir?" And he said, "I am a poltergeist." So I was naturally very pleased and I said, "That is splendid news. I have always wanted to meet a poltergeist, so if you are agreeable we will go and drink beer at the Dutch Club." And we did and you will never guess who it was.'

I had already guessed. Adrian, of course. I had given him some account of Erik and he had recognised him at once. Not surprisingly. There couldn't be two people looking like Erik.

We were always pleased to see Erik appear. Or almost always. Dutton was giving a dinner party one evening - a very superior affair. It may have been for, his Commanding Officer. For the life of me, I can't think how I came to be among the guests but I was. We were sitting around making sedate conversation and using the finger bowls when Erik lurched into the room - he never remembered to knock or ring unless he found the door bolted.

'Ah, you are already eating? Never mind. You need not worry about me. Go on with your meal. I have here something which I will eat in your company.'

From one pocket he extracted a bottle of beer, from the other a misshapen object wrapped in a sheet of dirty newspaper. From this, in turn, he brought out a grisly chunk of rabbit. Seating himself uninvited among us nobs he proceeded to worry the carcase with loud exclamations of satisfaction, pausing only to lift the beer bottle to his lips. When, in a silence broken only by the sound of bones being crunched (the larger ones he laid delicately on the tablecloth), he had finished his feast, he wiped his mouth with the back of his hand and began an eloquent discourse on the life and times of Lautreamont.

The C.O. left early.

Erik wasn't the only unusual solider around the place. There was Alf. Alf who? I'm not sure that I ever knew.

Standing next to Adrian and me at the bar of the Mitre one day was a singularly tough-looking larrikin in uniform. Various patches indicated that he had been in the Middle East - a sufficient warning that he'd been a good man not to get into a brawl with. Adrian, naturally, was unintimidated. He went on with whatever he was saying about Beowulf or the Minnesingers. I kept wishing to God he'd lower his voice. Not even his verbal witchery would cool this baby down if provoked.

Just as I'd feared, he suddenly swung round towards us. He looked grimmer full-face than he had in profile.

'Balls, mate - yer talking balls.' I got ready to run. 'What I reckon, those galahs that did the Beowulf stuff, they weren't out to make bloody poetry. All they bloody cared about was making up a good yarn. The bloody poetry just sort of got added on.'

That was Alf. He spoke as if he'd never been to school and if he had it certainly wasn't Geelong Grammar. He was Ocker to his fingertips to look at him or to hear his grating voice you would have thought that he'd have trouble reading a comic strip and that his only interest was two-up or the dogs. And here he was telling Adrian all about Beowulf. We soon discovered that he'd read plenty of other things, too. He never seemed to be at a loss whatever subject might crop up.

There was no way of finding out anything about him. His background, his occupation in civil life, what he hoped to do, the origin of his interest in literature - we couldn't get a word out of him. He refused our suggestions that he should meet Deasey or Dutton or Erik. 'Nah, sounds like a nice bloke but I don't reckon I'll come with yer. Knock back a couple of beers with yer at the boozer tomorrer, if yer like.'

Alf saw to it that we were treated with due respect when in his company. During one session at the Mitre, a couple of ill-disposed acquaintances at the further end of the bar eyed Adrian and me with pronounced hostility. I don't remember who they were - perhaps they were both Noel Counihan. As they set up their habitual litany about anti-Soviet scum and all the rest of it, Alf became restless. 'Reckon I'd better put a stinger under the tails of those bunnies,' he said. It wasn't worth it we told him. They'd pipe down when they started to get hoarse. That wasn't Alf's way. 'Listen, yer bloody drongos,' he bellowed, 'just keep it up for another bloody minute and I'll tear yer bloody balls off. Yer get the idea?' They got the idea.

He was too good to last. We arrived at the Mitre one day to knock back a couple of beers and there was no Alf. We never saw him again.

Then there was Bernard. Everyone has become so vilely respectable that it would certainly cause a touch of embarrassment if I were to give his real name so Bernard it is, although Beverley or Cecil would be much more appropriate. We'd been at the same school but he was several years older than I so we had never had any contact. If I'd been prettier I'm fairly confident that Bernard would have pranced gracefully across the generation gap and done his best to arrange a very close contact indeed. None of us urchins had the least doubt about his proclivities. He looked like a dissipated Abraham Lincoln minus the beard, if such a thing can be imagined, and he was the most unabashed homosexual I ever came across. He was also (which, I'm well aware, doesn't necessarily follow) the most gleefully effeminate. Once I heard him explaining to a friend why he always entered the school races. Such athletic activities m his part seemed wildly incongruous. Besides, his friend said in honest puzzlement, he always came last. 'But, my dear, I *want* to come last. That's the whole *idea*. All the time I'm trundling along in the rear, I have the most *delicious* view of those twinkling buttocks in front.'

Bernard, of course, planned lo be an actor. When he left school he went off to England. I don't think he was much of a success on the stage. I'm sure he was a huge success off it. After a year or two he came back to Australia. One day I found myself standing next to him in a pub. It seemed silly lo pretend I didn't know who he was.

'Aren't you Bernard So-and-so?'

'I think so. And you? Oh, do say you're a fan.'

'I've never seen you on the stage but we were at school together.'

'Oh, what pranks we could have got up to if I'd known you then.'

Adrian came into the bar, looking bedevilled. I introduced them.

'Goodness,' said Bernard gazing ecstatically at Adrian's ravaged and tormented face, 'I think you're the bonniest thing I've ever seen. I'd like lo drench you in Chanel.'

This was the only occasion when I saw Adrian momentarily taken aback. But only momentarily. He rallied strongly.

'I'd smell like a chanel house.'

Bernard had something of Adrian's own mystifying ability to create hazardous situations and emerge from them unscathed. Adrian, as I mentioned earlier, could talk in pubs and cafes and trams and buses - and in no undertone, either -

about Debussy and the Minnesingers and Henry James and get away without a scratch. Anyone else would have been judged guilty of coming the raw prawn and the consequence would have been at best some very dirty looks and possibly threats of physical reprisals.

In the same way, surrounded in a pub by a throng of toughs on their way home from a football match and already half stinking, Bernard could carry on like the Queen of the Fairies and come to no harm whatever. He would be wearing the sort of clothes which alone should have been enough to get him slugged - he had some wonderful flowered waistcoats, I remember, and his bow ties were fairly asking for trouble. Half-a-yard of silk handkerchief trailed from his breast-pocket. His shoes were suede which in those days was considered an open avowal of depravity. He called shrilly for his favourite drink - a loathsome deep purple liqueur called *Parfait Amour*. There might be a few bellicose rumblings on his first entry but his untroubled air, his complete serenity, somehow calmed everyone down in a matter of minutes. The glances he got from the beefy drinkers surrounding him became almost affectionate. Bernard would take ceremonious leave of them. 'Oh, this dear, *dear* maleness! I do *hate* to cast you aside, you sweet things! But I simply must *run*!'

When the war broke out Bernard got ready to fight - fight, that is, to keep out of the army. He pleaded work of national importance ('Those dear troops need us mummers, nothing like the playhouse for sending morale sky high'), neurasthenia, conscientious objection on religious grounds, sole support of an aged mother and, for all I know, housemaid's knee. It worked pretty well for quite a time but the army got him in the end.

He was only in the militia, of course, which was charged exclusively with 'home defence'. Unfortunately, home turned out to include New Guinea. Bernard got there almost simultaneously with the Japanese. 'Poor old Bernard,' I said to myself, 'if he didn't suffer from neurasthenia before, he'll certainly be a textbook case by the time he gets back. Maybe he'll even go down with a genuine attack of housemaid's knee.'

Months went by with no news of him. I had grown to be really fond of the mad creature and hoped that he was somehow surviving. It was a relief when finally I heard his voice over the phone. 'My dear! It's the minstrel boy back from the wars. Aren't you glad? I'm on *leave,* my dear, and of course *panting* to see you again. Now don't pretend you've got anything else to do but come this *minute* to the Australia bar, we'll have a drinky-poo and I'll tell you all the gossip about New Guinea society. My *dear*, the way they go *on*!'

There was only one person in the bar when I arrived, a sergeant in jungle greens. It must be my imagination that he had strings of Mills bombs hanging all over him and that he was carrying a bazooka but that was the impression he conveyed. He could have been Alf's double. It was Bernard.

'Here you are, my sweet, and looking pretty as a picture! Isn't my costume a *dream*? Don't you *dare* say you don't like it. And my dear, I've been *wounded*! Fortunately, nowhere where it matters, if you know what I mean - and I'm sure you do, you saucy thing! Isn't it *hilarious*? I'm a *hero*!'

He was, too. Another friend who was also in Bernard's unit told me about it. Apparently the neurasthenic conscientious objector with housemaid's knee had practically overnight proved to be an efficient and courageous soldier. There was talk of giving him a DSM.

A city capable of producing an Alf and a Bernard and of leaving an Erik at liberty couldn't, I reflected, be wholly bad.

EIGHT

The war was over and we headed for the great outdoors - in other words, anywhere that wasn't Australia. There were some stay-at-homes. Adrian, for one, had no desire to move away. He was quite right. It would have made no difference. He carried his own firmament with him wherever he might happen to be. John Reed also stuck on, at 'Heidi', although the extended family he had laboriously engendered was beginning to dissolve. Still, there were other artists to be discovered and boosted, there was the Contemporary Arts Society to be kept puff-puffing along the rails he'd laid down for it. Melbourne needed him.

Angry Penguins had been added to the deathroll of Australia's cultural magazines but Max Harris, I think, remained behind to watch over the body. His travelling came later when I read, with respectful envy, an article tipping off his readers as to which of the world's great hotels could be patronised without loss of face. I could hardly believe that I'd once sloshed down beers with him in Melbourne's unlovely pubs.

Sid Nolan, I heard, was in Queensland, discovering himself. It would be some time before he tucked the Australian ethos into his portmanteau and carried it abroad, returning in due course to be a monument. Noel Counihan, somebody told me, had gone or was going to Japan. I resolved not to go to Japan. Most of us, in any case, favoured Europe. There was already a lot of politicians' babble about 'New Australians'. We were all set to be the New Europeans. This was looked on in those days as a perfectly respectable ambition the dangers of 'losing one's roots' hadn't yet been taken up by the intellectuals as one of their standard themes.

Some of the migratory flock left in a 'never again' frame of mind. Robert Close was one of these and, with what he'd had to put up with from cops and magistrates, it wasn't surprising. But, mostly, we wanted to get away simply because for so long it hadn't been possible to do so.

Not that it had become all that much easier since. The politicians and bureaucrats were scurrying about creating insoluble problems for the future and they couldn't be expected to do a satisfactory job unless they attended conferences in whatever cities could offer submissive call girls and plenty of grog.

They were so inflated with self-importance that they could have floated to their destination like Montgolfier balloons but they owed it to their position as accredited pests to clutter up the available means of transport. What with their secretaries, advisers, medical attendants, mistresses and miscellaneous hangers-on, there wasn't much space remaining for the riffraff. I spent months (as did everyone else who hadn't been appointed assistant to the Minister Plenipotentiary to Ulan Bator or spokesman for the Added Value Tax Committee) in pleading with shipping clerks to get me on to a catamaran or dugout canoe or anything else which could carry me to Europe.

The company which finally came through with the offer of a passage gave every indication of having previously been engaged in the transport of black ivory. Having switched to paying passengers, it was faced with the necessity of introducing some slight improvements in the travel conditions. All that was required of me was to sign a document whereby I agreed to sleep wherever I'd be least in the way, to eat whatever was put before me, and to make no complaint if I was beaten around the head with marlin-spikes or flogged with a rope's end. That company was taking no chances. And, as I soon discovered, rightly.

Adrian and Deasey came to the docks to see me off. They didn't get the opportunity. To make it clear that discipline would be enforced right from the outset, the hatches had been battened down. Nobody was allowed on board, nobody was allowed off. The two visitors retired disconsolately and Adrian (so Deasey later informed me) at once engaged a bunch of wharfies in a discussion of Middle English syntax and the Bauhaus. It took them a moment or two to tune in but once they did their attention was unwavering. They were very anxious that Adrian should let them know if there was any little thing he'd like them to steal for him from the next cargo they unloaded.

I would have done better to have waited until I could get a catamaran. The vessel on which I'd embarked with such insouciance was an unconverted troop ship and passengers enjoyed cozy accommodation in the hold. That document I'd signed had specified that the food would be plain but - was it 'acceptable'? Or 'adequate'? It would have been both to anyone who relished stews made out of hard tack and brackish water. We queued up docilely with tin trays into which the stuff was ladled by a scowling bucko mate. Liquor of any variety was prohibited. No doubt it was apprehended that, if sufficiently inflamed, we might break out of the hold and set the ship's officers adrift in a small boat.

The company couldn't have picked a better man than the captain to run this hell-ship. Whether he'd gained his experience in the slave trade or had been promoted from supervisor of the prison hulks, there's no way of knowing. Possibly both. Nobody ever laid eyes on him during the trip. He was merely a snarl coming over the ship's PA system. That was enough, though, to keep us cowering. Hunched one night in an obscure corner of the deck, I joined another sufferer in a discussion of the captain's weird propensity for treating us less as passengers than as captured stowaways. On the whole, we agreed, he had left nothing undone that could conduce to our discomfort - restricting the areas in which we were permitted to walk about, rationing the drinking water, arbitrarily ordaining Lights Out when the mood took him, ordering us to stay and swelter aboard when we were in port ... But even so, we speculated, were there perhaps one or two minor touches he'd overlooked?

'Life belts,' said my companion meditatively, 'life belts made of lead. There's a cry of "Man overboard!" Someone slings him a life belt and, as he reaches for it, it sinks like a stone. And how about this? As it sinks, it lights up and the last thing the drowning wretch sees is the words, "Ever been had?" ' And he went on to elaborate on the possibilities with a drollery and inventiveness that would have been a credit to Adrian himself, transforming our day-to-day miseries into an hilarious phantasmagoria, heaping one wild extravagance on top of another until the ship, the captain, our fellow passengers and the sea around us were fused into a mad gyrating universe. This, I reflected, agog with admiration, is pure surrealism. Talk about intuition!

Who could he be? In the expectation that he would reciprocate, I introduced myself.

'The poet?'

I wasn't accustomed to my name evoking any recognition and simpered accordingly.

'I read that poem of yours - *The Denunciad*. You really laid into everyone, didn't you?'

'Well, why not?'

'You were pretty rough on James Gleeson, I thought.'

'He probably deserved it. By the way, what's your name?'

'James Gleeson.'

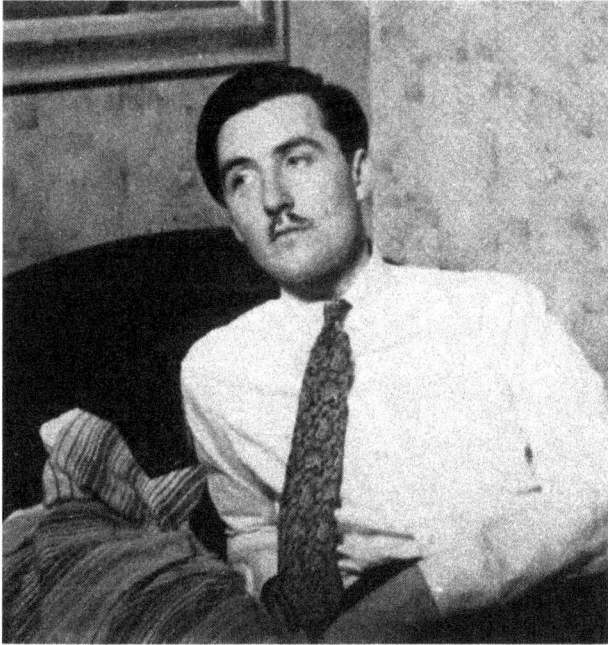

Top James Gleeson. *Above* Tucker with Joy Hester.

A slight pause ensued. I was wondering whether I'd take the coward's way out and jump over the rail. To be pent up with both a resentful artist and a psychotic captain was rather more than I could face. Jimmy enjoyed my consternation for a moment and then laughed without malice. From then on, that voyage to the end of the night was not merely bearable, it was a delight.

I kept recalling those pre-war posters for Mediterranean cruises - brilliantined heads (with here and there a distinguished touch of grey), disdainful ladies, everyone in evening dress and tucking into caviar. That isn't how it was on our twentieth-century Bounty. We were a ruffianly lot down in the hold, not a pot of caviar between us. There was a professional boxer in the next bunk to mine who started the day as he meant to go on by being seasick. For reasons they never made clear, there was a bunch of footballers heading for new horizons. A couple of journalists kept making notes for the articles they planned to write about Captain Bligh, the food, the bunks, the brackish drinking water and the caulking of the seams. Those articles, they told us, were going to make Zola's *J'accuse* look like the award of a Nobel Prize. And James Gleeson wasn't the only painter on board. There was Noel Wood who normally (if that's the word) led a Gauguin existence on an island in the Barrier Reef.

'Pretty lonely, isn't it?'
'No, I love it.'
'It'd scare the hell out of me.'
'I was only scared once. That was during the war.'
'The Japanese army getting too close?'
'No. The Australian army.'

Noel had had to go to the mainland to pick up supplies. It was just then the first troops were brought back from the Middle East. Ambling along the main drag, he heard the sound of an approaching convoy. A long line of open trucks bearing alarmingly seasoned warriors appeared. Noel, bearded and sandalled, looked every inch a civilian. How would the approaching tough eggs react? Would they merely attack him verbally? Or would they feel that he was a case for beating up? He looked anguishedly around. There was nowhere to hide. The first truck drew level with him. A great shout went up. Here, thought Noel, commending his soul to God, it comes. It came all right.

'Jesus Christ! Look at that! A dinkum bloody civilian! Good on yer, mate! Haven't seen one of you buggers for years! You little beauty!'

Truck after truck went by and the same enthusiastic cries came from each of them. If General Blamey had ever had anything like the same reception from the troops, Noel assured us, he would have felt like Napoleon reviewing the old Guard.

Land ho! Only not for us. We'd put in at one or two ports, had licked our chops at the prospect of getting off the slave galley and had ended up staring bleakly at the coast. Blackbeard wasn't prepared to let us go. He liked us to be where he could keep an eye on us. Finally, we docked at Bombay. We were to be there for a week. Presumably, the Captain decided that if we didn't get something other than hard tack to eat we might go down with scurvy and he'd have all the trouble of burying us at sea. With a sharp warning over the PA system that it was a privilege not a right, we were granted shore leave. If we'd been anything like serious-minded, I suppose we would have paid a visit to the Parsee Towers of Silence or whatever other sites were on the prescribed list for respectable travellers. We might even have sought the company of militant members of the Congress Party and had some earnest conversations. What did we do? We went and had a drink. Beer had been practically unobtainable in Australia during the war. The Captain wasn't going to have any drinking on *his* ship, thank you. We were thirsty.

The place for sahibs like us, we were told by an affable taxi-driver, was the Taj Mahal. Not the one in Noel Coward's *Private Lives* that didn't look like a biscuit box. This Taj was Bombay's most glittering hotel. Perhaps Max in his mature appraisal of the world's great hotels doesn't place the Taj among the joints that the right sort of people go to. I don't know. It suited us all right.

Us, on this occasion, meant James Gleeson, a couple of other painters, a professional footballer (he never told us what witchery England had for footballers), a boxer ... but I can't remember everyone of those who made up our parched, thank-gadding group. The Raj was still running things and we were treated with a deference to which the Mitre and the Four Courts and Richardson's hadn't accustomed us. Not that we cared. The waiters could have belted us over the ears as long as they gave us something to drink.

There was a remarkably alluring Swedish girl on the ship. I'd glimpsed her from afar - afar because she was one of the select, a cabin passenger, and the Captain wouldn't allow cabin passengers to be contaminated by scum of our sort. A rope had been strung across the deck to keep us from making a nuisance of ourselves to our betters. We crossed it at our peril. Now, the ravishing Swede came swaying deliciously into the Taj. We invited her to join us. She accepted. All the way from Melbourne to Bombay, she'd had access to such delights as unlimited bathwater, edible food and a bed instead of a bunk. But she too, she told us, had had enough of shipboard life. Until we set off again, she proposed to stay at the Taj. Why, I asked myself in a spasm of lubricity, shouldn't I stay at the Taj, too? Would that be a good idea? I did. And it was. Expensive though. Deasey, in addition to paying my fare, had shoved a hundred pounds at me just before I left. 'Here you are, Al. You might need it. Pay me back out of your first best-seller.' He would never have got his money back, poor Deasey, if he'd waited for that. Meantime, I had a hundred pounds. Had *had* a hundred pounds, because I returned to the ship with no regrets but with no money either.

So what, I wondered fearfully as I prepared to disembark at Southampton, was the next step? It looked as if it would take me straight into a doss house. No money, no job, no 'contacts', no - but there was Dutton. He'd made a break for it before any of us. He was installed in Oxford, an undergraduate. I went to Oxford. It was a circus in those days. Most of the students, like Dutton himself, were ex-servicemen, loyally determined in spite of their age and background to observe the old traditions. There was something simultaneously touching and absurd about the sight of a former submarine commander scrambling over a wall because he'd got back to college after the appointed hour. Or a much-decorated air force pilot scuttling to escape the proctors.

But Dutton's presence in England was a bit of luck for me. For the first penurious weeks in England, I bedded down on the floor of his exiguous flat, drank whatever liquor he had in stock, jeered at his membership of the college eight, reminisced about Sid and Max and *Angry Penguins*, met his undergraduate friends - one of whom, the American writer George Bailey, was to become a lifelong friend of my own- and from time to time speculated uneasily about what would happen when Dutton decided that enough was enough.

Albert Tucker in 1951, camped on the banks of the Seine in a caravan he built in his Paris hotel room.

What happened (although Dutton, with god-like forbearance, never did throw me out) was that I went to Paris. There were escapees there too. Bert Tucker was living on the Left Bank. We met now and again but not as often as I would have liked. I still regret that I wasn't able to observe his feat of building a caravan in the none too roomy room he occupied, lowering the components via the window for assemblage on the street below.

David Strachan had his studio in Montparnasse, just around the corner from the cheap hotel (superlatively cheap since for months on end I couldn't pay the bill) where my then wife and I were living. Throughout the time I knew him, David affected a somewhat languid air; but in reality he possessed an impressive ability to work tirelessly and single-mindedly. Currently, he was preoccupied with deep colour etching and was anxious to produce a book with illustrations of his own using this technique. I was elated when he proposed to use some poems of mine as a pretext for the book and more elated still when I saw the finished product. It was (not that I'm inviting anyone to admire the poems) one of the most spectacularly sumptuous volumes ever produced anywhere, certainly the most perfect book ever conceived and executed by an Australian.

He was a contradictory fellow, David. Just as those world-weary mannerisms of his were a cover-up for his enthusiasm and energy, so his lethal wit was accompanied by a readiness to help anyone he liked. Back in Australia my wife and I had agreed that no writer, painter or composer had ever produced work worth a damn until he'd put in a ritual spell of starving in Paris.

When we found ourselves doing just that we were ready to exchange the world's entire cultural output for a ham sandwich.

Somehow or other, David heard that we were getting peckish and, in addition, were what French officialdom menacingly terms *sans domicile fixe.* With no trace as he made the offer of 'see what a good boy am I', he told us that he was shortly leaving for Spain and that we could have his studio while he was away. He'd hardly caught his train before we moved in. The place was so full of food it looked like a supermarket. There was a note perched on top of these goodies instructing us to make pigs of ourselves. We did; and if I thereby bitched my chances of ever writing a line worth reading, the hell with it.

Whenever she could, Alannah Coleman would make her getaway from England and pay us a visit. She no longer wore a fez or carried a quiver of arrows but she was as decorative as ever. Dutton, too, would turn up every so often, and, on an average of once a week, or so it sometimes seemed, congenial compatriots - the artist Geoff Jones or the philologist Sid Baker - whom I'd never known in Australia would appear on the scene. Australian exiles were in abundant supply. There was no risk of homesickness.

Nobody had heard from Deasey. Presumably he was still among the stay-at-homes. Now and again I wondered what he was up to. Only now and again, though. I was busy. I was twenty-five years old. What keeps a twenty-five-year-old busy? Writing a novel, of course, that inescapable autobiographical novel. It was easy. One was a fascinating creature oneseif and one's friends provided the other characters. What are friends for?

My novel featured them all - Adrian and Deasey and Dutton and Max and anyone else I'd ever known. I'd written some great dialogue for the Deasey character - better than the original. '*Jaysus*! I've taken someone else's car. It *looked* like mine.' That - or something equally brilliant - was what I'd written one day when I decided to go out for a drink. I left the sheet in the typewriter. I came back an hour or so later and glanced at my typescript. 'Jaysus! I've taken someone else's car. It *looked* like mine. Let's hope there aren't any bloody tarantulas in it. That's the trouble with Bentleys - full of tarantulas.'

My trouble was that I hadn't written the last two sentences. I'd had a few drinks but not all that many and I distinctly remembered that I'd broken off at 'the same as mine'. What, in God's name, was going on?

I found out later that evening. Without bothering to let anyone know, Deasey had followed the mass migratory movement and come to Paris. Somehow he had persuaded the concierge (he had a French vocabulary of about six words at the time which made this achievement nothing short of miraculous) to let him into my room, had naturally read everything lying around, and had decided to add a note of authenticity to the dialogue I'd invented. My nervous twitching stopped quite soon but it had been a spooky moment.

Apart from Adrian, it was Gino's absence from the expatriate gang in Paris which we most regretted. He'd left Australia (what on earth could Melbourne be like without the Leonardo?) but was living in Rome. It took some time for Australians like ourselves to appreciate that you could actually reach a foreign country without spending six weeks on a boat. When this had finally sunk in, a visit to Gino became imperative.

His new bookshop, the 'Quattro Venti' in Via della Scrofa, had previously offered its customers an alluring selection of missals, bibles and the works of St Thomas Aquinas. Gino, of course, had eliminated these scandalous publications but members of the clergy, unaware of the change of policy, were constantly dropping in to pick up a breviary or something and the sight of Gino on these occasions, his natural courtesy contending with his aversion for such witch doctors, was always a treat.

He was glad to see us, not perhaps so much for our bright eyes as because we were a reminder of Melbourne. Desmond O'Grady in his article confirms what I felt straight away - that Gino rather regretted having quit Australia. He talked with evident nostalgia of Adrian, of Bert (He organised a show of Bert's paintings at the 'Quattro Venti'), of Max, even of John Reed. The rest of us looked back - and down - on Melbourne as provincial. Gino, on the contrary, found Rome provincial.

It took me a long time to see that he had a point. I never got around to thinking that Paris and Rome were, as Gino in his more extreme moments was inclined to suggest, mere backwaters. But I did come around to realising that there had been a liveliness, a degree of energy and enthusiasm in Melbourne during the *Comment* and *Angry Penguins* years which was somehow lacking elsewhere. Paris was an exciting city. The people in it, the writers and painters at least, were a bit tepid compared to their counterparts in Australia, in Melbourne. Once upon a time we'd hankered sentimentally after cafe terraces. Now I had the terraces but something was missing.

INDEX